THE VILLAGE
OF MY CHILDHOOD

THE VILLAGE
OF MY CHILDHOOD

Fred Archer

ALAN SUTTON
1989

ALAN SUTTON PUBLISHING
BRUNSWICK ROAD · GLOUCESTER

British Library Cataloguing in Publication Data

Archer, Fred, *1915–*
    The village of my childhood.
    1. Hereford and Worcester. Ashton-under-hill.
    Social life, history
    I. Title
    942.4'49

ISBN 0-86299-557-4

Jacket picture: Saturday Afternoon by A.S. Gunning King, Bradford City Art Gallery and Museums (*Photograph: The Bridgeman Art Library*)

Colour Illustrations 1 and 6 from The Bridgeman Art Library.
Colour Illustrations 2, 3, 4, 5, 7 and 8 from Fine Art Photographic Library Ltd.

352690
942.449

Typesetting and origination by
Alan Sutton Publishing Limited
Printed in Great Britain by
Dotesios Printers Limited

Contents

CONTENTS

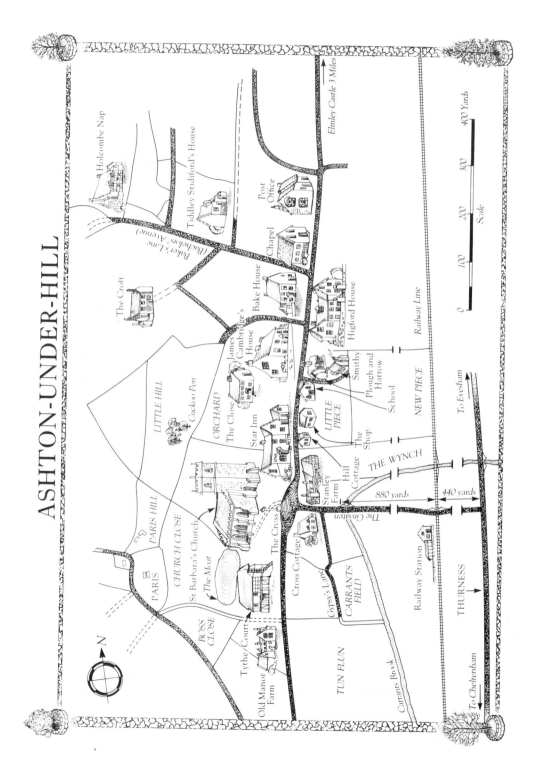

ASHTON-UNDER-HILL

1

The Village of Ashton-under-Hill

Between the Cotswolds and the Malverns lies the Vale of Evesham where the River Avon winds through the fertile black loam of the market gardens. Rising from the Vale is that outcrop of the Cotswolds, Bredon Hill, known as The Stranded Whale, where the hawthorn hedges are replaced by dry-stone walls and where the elms of the Vale, lately gone, give way to beech trees, larch and firs. Under Bredon Hill, to the east, is the village of Ashton where I was born in 1915, the village of my childhood.

Ashton still takes its shape from the long village street which snakes northwards along the foot of Bredon Hill towards Elmley Castle. On either side of the street stand solid, stone farmhouses; ancient black and white half-timbered cottages; handsome houses of Georgian and Victorian times; brick terraces. At the south end of the street a lych-gate and a row of drooping ash trees, a copper beech towering over a yew, lead to the Church. The footpath passes the tombstones which bear so many Ashton names, the gleaming water of the moat, and leads on up through Church Close and its old oaks to the lower slopes of Bredon.

In the village street in front of the Church stands a fifteenth-century cross. In years past its stone steps have been worn by politicians, preachers, the village children; by old men resting there to smoke their clay pipes and talk of even earlier times. From the Cross the street winds its leisurely way along to the Chapel at the other end of the village, past buildings and trees which stood there long before I was born.

Yet the Ashton that I knew as a child has gone for ever. I grew up in the 1920s, the son of a well-to-do farmer, when the village was a self-contained community of three hundred people, most, rich or poor, depending on the land for their livelihood, as their parents and grandparents had before them. In those days market gardening was spreading to the heavy clays

1

The ancient black and white cottages and stone houses of the village of Ashton-under-Hill

around Ashton, replacing the fields of grain with sprouts and peas, but there were still cattle and sheep and both farmers and market gardeners needed manpower and horsepower to work the fields and to harvest the crops. Very few travelled outside the village to work. Even the newcomers, like the ironmaster James Cambridge who travelled to Birmingham every day, had their stake in the land, their fields and orchards.

With my brother and some of the other boys from the village, I travelled every day on the train to Evesham, first to the Preparatory School and then to the Grammar School. But most of the village children were taught at the village school. We all helped on the land well before our formal schooling was finished.

Before the service bus and the motor car, when the last train left Evesham at seven in the evening, we still led the parochial existence of our grandparents' day. The village shop, the Post Office Stores and the local tradesmen's carts provided most of the villagers' needs. If there was time for recreation, it could be taken in one of the two pubs or at the Recreation Room. Our grandparents too would have felt at home in our world of

Ashton children on the fifteenth-century village cross

paraffin lamps and candles, earth closets and chamber pots. Only the most progressive had septic tanks ('dumb wells' the villagers called them) for WCs and baths or, like Mr Cambridge's son, an engine and dynamo to light the house with electricity.

For most people the village was their world. But Ashton was so unimportant to the world outside that it did not even have its own vicar or policeman. They both lived at Beckford, a neighbouring village worthy of a signal box and where the joint funeral bier was kept. If anyone was a bit above himself people would say, 'Thee hast bin to Beckford.'

THE VILLAGE STREET

For generations the roads were a meeting place in the village. When the water was fetched from the standpipe or pump, people stood and talked.

In the early 1920s there were about three cars in our village and the only goods traffic not horse-drawn was the DCL Yeast van on its way to Mr Stallard, the baker, and the Brooke Bond Tea Trojan chain-drive van going to Mrs Collins' shop. Little did I think that fifty years later I'd be looking both ways twice before crossing the road. In those days I saw a busy road not of motor traffic but people, animals, to and fro from morning until night.

The baker's cart meets a farm cart in a village lane

An villager standing at his cottage door

The cows came up from Tun Flun (Ten Furlongs Field) in the early light in spring. They followed a hurricane-lamp in the dark winter before dawn. Horses walked nose to tail, haltered on the way to the stable and breakfast; on early summer mornings carters and ploughboys rode their horses side-saddle to the hayfields. The men, breeched, gaitered and hobnail-shod, all left home at six forty-five, often carrying with them their lunch in a straw frail basket, their tea cans, and the daylabourers their spades, bill hooks, shuppicks (pitchforks), hoes and the simple tackle they required for the day's work.

Then later the postman came on his carrier bike from Evesham with the letters. The baker's cart stopped and the baker attached the reins to a hook in the front of his covered cab.

Ladies on sit-up-and-beg cycles with dress guards rode to and from the shop, the baker and the Post Office. I watched with delight as I stood by the pub wall with Frank Davis to see Jasper Hill mount his polished Raleigh bike, by scooting along with one foot on the rear hub step until he had got up enough speed to vault on to the saddle.

To walk the road to school in an ordinary way was unusual. The village boys and girls bowled their hoops made from drill wheels, whipped their tops, leap-frogged or walked on stilts made from the ash coppice.

Everyone's hens fetched their grit from the road. Goats were tethered on the grassy banks and outside the houses.

Some Saturday mornings, I watched our cows and kept them in bounds as they pulled the fresh green spring grass from the wider strips, the roadside, the hedge. Joe Baker carried his candle lantern to Chapel Sunday nights and left it in the porch. He was a great walker, and always seemed happy with a wheelbarrow as he went to his allotment during the summer evenings.

At half past five in the evening, after a day behind the plough or harrow when the clay clung to the boots, the men walked home along the village street scuffing their boots on the road, always carrying something. The frail was now empty of food and drink but filled with wood chips and spawls from the fallen tree, or occasionally a rabbit for late dinner the next day caught by a dog or (who knows?) a wire snare.

I remember Walt Davis, after he had taken a dray-load of fruit to market, walking past our house carrying a log for the fire.

The green fields were a good place to be in summer, but even then the hard road to the cottage door and tea-time was a happy place.

Men with ferrets going rabbiting on Bredon Hill

GARDENS AND BACKYARDS

In summer-time after tea, everybody was busy in the vegetable garden among the potatoes, the beans and the cabbages. The more ambitious grew onions of enormous size for the local shows and the pig in the backyard sty ate all that the family left over. In those days, vegetables were a vital product of the cottage gardens. Only a few flowers were grown — forget-me-nots, roses, columbines and sweet peas, phlox and night-scented stock. Clematis or rambler roses around the larch porches brightened up the heavy-hinged front doors, generally painted a dull brown.

The backyards of the cottages were busy places. Here were the washhouse and the privy, the pigsty and the shed. Here the firewood was split, and all the tools, used in their season, were hung up: hoes, sickles, scythes, a breast plough for the allotment, a pig-bench and ladder for pig-killing, and the bath for Friday nights.

On Mondays, a fire of slack coal, sprout stems, old shoes and any other household rubbish, roared under the copper boiler in the washhouse. As the steam rose in clouds, the washing was boiled white in soap, soda and Reckitt's blue to be hung on the wire clothes line in the backyard.

In orange-box cages, the villagers kept wild birds, rescued perhaps as fledgelings, most so tame that they roamed at will. There was a jackdaw which always said, 'Morning, hello,' to me whatever the time of day, and a magpie which would perch on my shoulder until I gave him his usual biscuit, flying off to eat it and calling, 'Thank you,' from the top of the washhouse.

Some cottages kept goldfinches, caught somehow in the thistle blows on Bredon Hill; some said it was by Oliver Hampton using birdlime (that illegal sticky substance which traps birds by their feet). Goldfinches were kept for their song, and for crossing with canaries.

Other boxes held exotic breeds of rabbits, which we set free to join the wild rabbits of Bredon Hill when their cages became too overcrowded. And there were ferrets. Oliver showed me the bundles of cream fur which were the latest litter, while in another cage, the hob (the male) clawed at the wire for his food; I can still recall his pungent smell.

BROOKS AND BRIDGES

Our village, being at the foot of the hill, has an abundant supply of water oozing out of the slopes. One such stream is Holcombe Brook, flowing from

A visitor to the village on one of the footbridges over Carrants Brook

the Big Wood, past the badger earths, the coppice where the aconite and bluebell make their carpets in the spring, and down in the Vale. At right angles to Holcombe Brook, as it passes through the field 'Big Holbrook', there runs a ditch under a row of stunted elms. Nothing unusual about this except that the ditch runs two ways. The land, falling to north and south, makes the water which goes north follow the parish boundary to Hinton and empty into the Avon at Evesham. The part of the ditch which flows south joins Holcombe Brook which runs into Carrants Brook, winding sluggishly to join the Avon at Tewkesbury.

Carrants Brook is the one closely connected with our village. A watering place for cattle, with withy trees, both common and red, lining its banks, watercress growing at the sides and a few eels living in the deeper parts. In winter it floods the meadows and the rabbits leave their holts in its banks and climb the hollow withy tree to lie high and dry in the roxy peaty tops, often covered with ivy and bramble. The wood pigeons feed on the ivy berries in winter. One or two fords exist where the cattle cross, but mostly the banks are steep with a mass of kingcups, ragged robin and meadow sweet, with its heady, rather sickly smell in high summer. The shade provides protection from the sun for the cows and the streams are alive with flies and insects of all kinds, including the occasional dragonfly.

St Barbara's Church and the moat

The brook has several bridges in the parish. The bridge in the Back Lane, or Gipsies Lane, is quite old and made of local stone. Hard by this bridge, a matter of fifteen yards away, there are the stone remains of a much earlier bridge for an ancient track known as 'Deviation Saltway', which was used in Roman times.

One bridge was especially dear to me. At the bottom of the First Ham, an L-shaped meadow, a large withy tree, ripe with age and split down the centre, lay on the edge of the brook. Half the tree, shaped like a half moon, had fallen across Carrants Brook and had taken root on the other bank, making an ideal natural bridge. We crossed and recrossed that bridge hundreds of times. In winter it was frightening as the waters rushed below, but in the summer it was the place to sit and catch an eel or two, or just a shady spot to watch life as it went on around us. When the brook was cleaned to improve the drainage of the hams, or water meadows, my little bridge had to go. It was slowing the progress of the water downstream to the Avon.

The stream through the orchard on our farm had not far to travel before it reached the brook; it is really just the overflow from the moat where as a lad I caught the occasional roach and set night lines for eels. Our moat is no ordinary moat. It lies in a hollow at the back of the Church where, in Church Close, the outline of the moated house, long since gone, is easily traced. The moat is really the monks' fishpond. Living about eighty miles from the sea, they depended on freshwater fish. The source is easily traced, the spring water boiling up out of the hill between two old oaks which seem ageless.

2

Memories of Home

BIRTH AND DEATH, ZEPPELINS AND SOLDIERS

At the end of April 1915, when village boys were dying in the Great War, I was born in Stanley Farm House, in Ashton-under-Hill.

While cousin Tom fought for 'The Old Country' in Flanders, a black-hooded photographer from Evesham took a photograph of me, a pudding covered with silk and lace, at seven months old. Then cousin Charlie's life was ended by a sniper's bullet in Mesopotamia soon after my first birthday.

Memories play tricks with the best of us, but I vividly remember hearing as a three-year-old the midnight call of Police Constable Smith as he stood in our front porch shouting, 'Zeppelins. Lights out!' Dark red curtains, the colour of a Hereford cow, were drawn over the bedroom window to keep the candle's glimmer indoors. Why Mr Smith came was a mystery to me, and so were Zeppelins.

As the war ended and I played in the pantry where the sacks of flour ground at Sedgeberrow Mill, the chest of tea, bars of lard and flitches of bacon were stored, I thought that all these things were commonplace in every house; I did not realise that they were an insurance against the submarine threat.

Months later came Armistice Day. Some of the village lads who had left in khaki returned in hospital blue and came home for good.

Mother encouraged us to wave little Union Jacks from the living room window when a trooper, putteed and spurred, walked smartly past. How foreign these men looked compared to the cow-haired, billycock-hatted men of the farm; now slouching with two buckets of milk yoked to their shoulders, or following the plough with a rolling gait like a drunken sailor. The straightness of the soldiers' backs put them head and shoulders above the workers of the field.

The author aged seven months

I pottered to the workshop where Grandad Westwood's carpenters' tools hung in neat rows against the beamed wall and watched him start on a wheelbarrow for me.

Grandad had rosy cheeks above his pointed beard, and his eyes were bright china blue. Although he was slightly built, I stood only just above knee-high to him in my pale green cotton knickers and blouse to match. I was still wearing sandal-type shoes with one strap and a button – my elder brother had graduated into lace-up boots.

When I did wrong and Dad put me across his knee, smacking hard at the green cotton knickers, Grandad said 'Not too hard, Tom, they be very thin.' I suppose Grandad Westwood was the first man to take my part as he dried my tears with his red spotted handkerchief and gave me a humbug.

I held tight to Grandad's hand one cold October morning when the pig was killed. The pig-killer, Joe Wheatcroft, would come to us every October as he came to the cottagers. The scene was like a ritual sacrifice. The squealing pig was held down on the pig-bench, then its squeals would suddenly stop as the knife went in. The bristles were burnt off by setting light to straw placed all over the carcass, even in the mouth, Joe skilfully moving the burning straw with his shuppick so that the skin wasn't burnt. Buckets of hot then cold water were used to scrub the pig white. Mother and Grandma bustled about carrying dishes of heart, liver and chitterlings into the kitchen. Then the pig, its empty belly propped open with a nut stick to the cold autumn air, was hung in the Back Place to be cut up next day, and Joe went into the House Place for the pig-killer's customary meal of a piece of liver fresh from the pig.

Then one morning my champion from the workshop was missing at breakfast. 'It's a cold on the chest,' Grandma said. Next morning he didn't come down the stairs, but the doctor, with his leather bag, called to see him. Sunday came and Grandma told us that Grandad had gone to live with Jesus and the Angels.

'But he won't be able to finish my barrow there,' I said.

'He's better there,' Mother said, 'he won't cough any more.'

The curtains were drawn as I passed the bedroom window on my way to Sunday School, and that afternoon Aunty Polly came from Beckford and Dad drove us over in the governess cart to stay a few days with her and Uncle Joe. That was us two boys, my baby sister stayed at home with Mother.

When we came back, Grandad's chair stood empty with its red cushion. The wooden arms were worn slightly by the grip of his fingers and thumbs over the years.

I said my prayers each night in front of the oven grate at Grandma's knee. Grandma sat in a winged easy chair between the fire and the clock. She was stout, and she prompted me over the words 'Pity my simplicity'. In the evenings she wore a navy silk dress decorated with white lace and mother of pearl buttons on the sleeves. On a thin chain around her neck was a golden locket which she opened to show me a photograph of Grandad when he was young.

The soldiers were still returning from the trenches of France. Often ten minutes after a train stopped at our little station, some son of Ashton walked past towards home.

Sometimes I went to Evesham with Tom and Mother and the baby in the governess cart. Ponto, who slept in a waggon in the cart shed, harnessed the pony – a chestnut called Polly – and with the shining brasses and the smell of leather we snuggled down on the upholstered seats of the cart. Dad sat at the back by the door, the reins lying across a brass bracket on the front. At a click of Dad's tongue, Polly trotted down the Groaten past the station and over the bridge to the main road. The war was over but German prisoners marched under escort over Sedgeberrow bank.

The journey to Evesham took about half an hour. Evesham was a place where markets were still held some days, and horses and drays, driven by cloth-capped market gardeners, mingled with the more sophisticated governess carts loaded with ladies sheltered by trap umbrellas, cane whips sticking out from the mudguard holders.

As the days lengthened in 1919, most of the fellows were wearing khaki jackets and puttees above their boots instead of the usual leggings as they followed the plough or harrowed the wheat, and preparations were made for the peace celebrations in Little Piece.

It was unusual for a boy of four to be out after dark in the village, but I was taken to see the huge bonfire and I picked up the rocket sticks as they landed on the field in Blacksmiths Lane. Aunty Lucy and Mrs Baker were not excited about the end of the war to end all wars. Their sons lay in the fields of France and Mesopotamia. Life for me was sheltered, even, tangible. For them it must have been bleak. Grandma would sigh as she sat in her wing chair, but she didn't give up her baking, tea-making, stew-jarring rabbits and hares.

I took my turn in the iron bath those far away Friday nights when the great iron pots swung from the pot-hooks to heat the bath water – hard water softened by Hudson's soap powder. The temperature of the water was tested by Mother's bare elbow and Mrs Hill, the char, blew her onion breath into my face as she towelled me dry.

Then came a dreadful epidemic of 'flu when half the village were laid low and several died. As our family went down like nine-pins, Dad sent for Aunty Lucy who came with all the interesting news and good intentions. She brought the medicine up to where I lay with my brother under the beams. Then, as we improved, she brought our two little mugs, one for my brother with the words 'For a good little boy' on it – mine read 'Think of me'.

As the 'flu passed and the last of the camphorated oil had oiled my chest, and the ipecacuanha wine had done its worst, men who had been ill and were 'on the box', (the box in which the Sick and Dividend Club funds were kept) walked in a sort of slow dawdle up and down our village street taking the air. They wore their Sunday go-to-meeting shoes; they held one hand, flat knuckles down, on the small of their backs. The urgency of daily work was laid aside. There seemed to me to be a special way of walking when you were on the box. Those who were off work had to be in by six.

Surely there was an art in all this, if only it was to prove to the able-bodied that they had been 'very middling', as they said, and now they were feeling 'pretty middling'.

In our rambling farmhouse where the only light was the yellow flame of the oil lamp, and where we each had our separate candles, a thunderstorm when the heavens opened and the whole landscape was lit by the lightning, was both wonderful and frightening.

'What was the noise in the night?' I asked Mrs Hill as she blackleaded the grate one morning.

'Just a moving the furniture up yonder in the sky, I reckon,' she said.

Grandma said it was God speaking to us. Then I asked Dad and he said it was two clouds hitting each other in the sky and making a noise and sending big sparks of lightning down.

'See God's promise in the orchard,' Grandma said. 'That's the rainbow. That means He will never flood the world again.' Then she told me about Noah's Ark. I ran through the trees making the ewes and lambs scatter as I chased the rainbow when the rain had stopped. Bonnie and her foal stopped grazing and stared. I was sure the rainbow was settled on the Hay plum tree near the hedge, but when I got there it was gone. I tried to catch the next one by the withies near the stream, but that went again.

Then Grandma died in her sleep in the blue room from which Grandad had seen the apple blossom for the last time.

THE HOUSE AND THE BACK PLACE

Our living room was a mixture of kitchen and sitting room. It was always known as The House. The cooking was done there on the black-leaded grate. All meals were served there except on Sundays when we either went into the little dining room, where the fire smoked for years because a sweep left his brush up the chimney, or into the drawing room which had been renovated.

Beyond The House lay the Back Place. An L-shaped, blue-coloured stone-slabbed floor where the huge timbers flaked with whitewash. Mrs Hill spent her time here at the brown salt-glazed sink or at one of the two copper boilers. The sack of kibbled maize in the corner was usually good for a rat when Dad moved it for Rip, the Airedale-cross fox terrier. There was a churchy smell about the Back Place; musty, damp. The sway over the fireplace had two pot-hooks from which hung an iron pot almost like a gipsy cauldron. Mrs Hill, I imagined, was brewing some secret potion in that

Stanley Farm with the author's mother, father, sister Clarice and Rip the dog

pot, but in fact it was often a ham, something too big to cook in The House. She prepared the vegetables out there, then carried them into The House for cooking. The two copper boilers side by side were stoked on Mondays with slack coal. One furnace, as we called it, was for the washing and next to it stood the dolly tub and a huge mangle. The other furnace was used for cooking small potatoes in their jackets for the pigs. When the wooden, rounded lids were raised by Mrs Hill, she could vaguely be seen in a cloud of steam stirring the washing with a stick or lifting it into the dolly tub. The smell of Sunlight soap and wet flannel filled the Back Place.

In the inglenook, sides of bacon yellowed as they dried straight from the salting lead. Backbone chines from the last pig hung from hooks in the whitewashed rafters. To the left of the back door was a plain corner cupboard, too high for me to reach. In it lay the mysteries of treating ailing farm animals. Turpentine, linseed oil, Cataline, Stockholm tar, sweet nitre, green oils, white oils, raddle for marking sheep – Dad's medicine cupboard when carter, cowman or shepherd needed these things. Another shelf was packed with calf powders for white scour, ringworm ointment, udder salve, fresh liquor. Then there were the twitches to put on horses, marking irons for sheep and cattle and Pettifers Mixture – a tonic for most things.

A row of coat pegs in plain wood stuck out like half a ladder inside the door. Here hung the outdoor working clothes and Dad's spare leather belt. He used this to carry the wicker peck baskets up the ladders when he was fruit picking, and to tan my hide when necessary.

This was the Back Place. Coldish in winter except near the fire, and cool in summer. Little Mrs Hill nipping around in her harden apron charring, as it was called. She smelt of onions and eucalyptus. She wore steel-rimmed spectacles. Her hands were rough, her face red. It was here she picked the fowls, dressed them, put the eggs into boxes. This was her headquarters. One thing Mrs Hill did every morning was to boil an iron pot of water which George Bendalls fetched to wash out the milk churns and scald his milk buckets.

I liked Mr Bendalls. He played his tin whistle to me in the cooling shed. Always hymns. He was strong Chapel. Sometimes he sang as he milked the cows. His greasy cap was pushed by his grey-haired head deep into each cow's flank as he sat on the three-legged stool, made by Oliver Hampton, the three-gallon bucket between his corded knees. The milk almost sang into the pail as his accompaniment.

I see the Back Place as a little power-house of both the farm and house. I used to sit and listen to Dad, Mr Carter, his partner, and Mr Bendalls as they looked so serious sitting round the fire some winter evenings when Mrs Hill had gone home.

They were waiting for a cow to calve in the Lidded Place – a sort of sick bay against the cowshed. Every so often they went across the yard with their hurricane lanterns to see how things were going. Then the shepherd would come for Dad or Mr Carter to help him lamb a ewe, or Walt to discuss the working of the land for the early peas.

To potter after Mr Bendalls in the cow yard, meet Shepherd Corbisley with Dad in the sheep pens or sit on the stable bench suited me; there was always something interesting going on. But, at five years old, I had my old grey jersey packed away for Saturdays, my sailor suit had to be laid aside and off we went to Gloucester by train to buy clothes.

Dad was particular that the flannel knickers, as they were called, were big enough for next year. He bought a navy blue blazer with an enormous EPS badge sewn on it which meant Evesham Preparatory School. A pair of lace-up black boots replaced my shoes and galoshes and with a fawn raincoat and navy cap with another great red badge, a satchel and pencil case, I was ready to join my brother on the eight-fifty train to Evesham.

18

The author's mother and father, Tom and Lily Archer

So parochial was life in 1920 that the head teacher detected a Gloucestershire accent in me; Evesham was Worcestershire, Ashton in those days was not.

I enjoyed being taught by the motherly infants' teacher how to make pothooks with the pencil, but home was best.

THE SIGHTS AND SOUNDS OF HOME

Home to me as a child meant most of all my mother. Mother adapted herself to the day, unhurriedly active. When Mrs Hill had done the morning's housework, trimmed the brass oil lamps, breathed hard on the glass globe and polished it with a duster until it shone, Mother would be ironing on the kitchen table. Heating the irons on the trivet of the oven grate. Then, before tea, she would arrange the pokerwork mats on the sideboard.

The afternoon light shone on the pink glass ornaments in the whatnot and on the glass droppers. I saw these in every aunt and uncle's house where I went Sunday visiting.

The grandfather clock gave a little warning note at about four minutes to

The author and his brother and sister, Tom and Clarice

five, then the clock struck and the tea was laid. At half past five when Dad arrived and sugared his tea, he'd give it a stir, then ladle a teaspoonful out of his cup, blow on it and taste it to see if it needed more sugar.

'Who started the loaf?' he would ask. Whoever it was, it was always started in the wrong place. 'Never mind,' he'd say, 'just remember another time.' A batch loaf must always be started in the right place, at the bulge. The spoon stood upright in the pot of egg plum jam and the butter made by Mrs Carter was good and plentiful.

In the winter, when the blinds were drawn, our living room soon warmed up with the heat of the fire and the oil lamps. The blinds were khaki-coloured oiled silk pulled down by a cord and fastened to the window sill. On the end of each cord was a wooden knob shaped like an acorn. Inside was the knot of the blind string. As an extra precaution from the cold the red tasselled curtain was drawn along the wooden-ringed track, completely blotting out the bay window.

Before bedtime in winter as Rip the terrier stretched out on the rag rug and the tabby cat purred away on the sofa, I sat in the inglenook under the shelf where Dad's twelve-bore cartridges were stacked, one hundred in a box, with the words 'Crimson Flash' along the side. As the wind howled in the chimney, big enough to hold Dad's cob and buggy, the soot fell like black snowballs into the tin where the small brick flue entered the square tower of chimney open to the stars.

A two-hundredweight sack of sprout seed stood dry in the corner. Here Dad scooped and weighed Archer and Carter's strain and posted it for £1 per pound. Then, like gold, hung another little seed bag labelled Robbin's Blue strain. A sprout variety bought from Evesham by Mr Carter. This was not for sale. Dad and Mr Carter talked of it in whispers. Precious seed.

The candles were lit, and after climbing the stairs, my brother and I were soon in bed. The brass knobs on the bedstead shone in the dim light of the candle. It never occurred to me that other boys went to bed in the same way. Seven o'clock. The sound of the church bells was welcome company in the dark and deserted village street. On whist-drive nights I heard the jolly knot of village folk walk past. One man had a wooden leg and it pounded on the road outside.

I could hear the stamping of horses' steel shoes on the cobbled stable floor down below us where the rats sharpened their teeth on the hard oak beams in the barn and drank from the dripping tap near the milk hut.

Morning came with the daily competition between the cocks from their withy perches among the fowls. Around the farms in our village, in the rickyards, the cowsheds and granaries, the hens scratched around the cockerels and the long spurred cocks strutted. They scratched the muck buries for worms, they obtained their grit from the village street, and, on a bare patch in our rickyard where the grass had been killed by the scratching over the years of our hundred or so fowl, we fed them twice a day, broadcasting the mixture – half wheat and half kibbled maize – calling the stragglers from their hiding places – bid, bid, bid, bid and whistling, as near as I remember, fee-oo, fee-oo, fee-oo. In winter time Dad cooked potatoes and fed them hot mashed with Sussex grown oats and a little spice. This was their morning breakfast. The fowl roosted at night in our old stone barn; the beams ran across the width of the roof and across those beams the fruit picking ladders were stored away for the winter.

First of all the hens flew up into the tallet and from there it was a mere flutter for them to reach the ladders. The more agile Anconas reached to the height of the barn while the stately Light Sussex cocks perched on the railings surrounding the calf pens. The hayloader just inside the barn, with its rows of lathes, looked as if it had been designed for one purpose – a hen roost on wheels.

Egg collecting was an exciting business. Sometimes we lay on our sides and reached them from an awkward spot under an old manger. This was fairly simple providing a broody hadn't decided to be sitting there.

It was dark under these mangers and I have put my hand on a hedgehog, but I was paid a penny a dozen for all eggs which I found that were not laid in the rows of pot hampers lined with hay in the dark corners under the tallet, the makeshift nesting-boxes.

Some laid in clumps of stinging nettles in the spring-time – no one thought of using sodium chlorate to destroy the nettles in those days just after the First World War. But what a pleasant surprise when a hen hatched her brood of chicks in such places. Dad and I would move the brood after dark, away from the rats, and perhaps a fox coming down off the hill. An old tea chest and a bit of wire and soon the mother hen was safe with her chicks and as we said 'she had stolen her nest'.

Sometimes I saw cousin George, who worked an extra team of horses from our stable, riding side-saddle with his plough-teams to the fields. Walt had the main lot of horses at Mr Carter's yard at old Manor Farm. George often took two to harrow or drill or plough the land by Great Hill Barn Land where the old men said the stones grew, because though they hauled them off every year for making cart roads, they never seemed to get any less. Everything seemed hurried with Mr Bendalls until he had seen his under cowman, Jim Earles, go station-wards with Min in the milk float with the great seventeen-gallon churns of milk. Then, after breakfast, they fed the calves, cleaned the shed up, while, up on the hill, Shepherd Corbisley had seen his sheep before the village street was aired. Winter and summer Walt foddered his horses at about half past five, but the shepherd alone saw the mist from the hill as it lay like a blanket along Carrants Brook.

As I walked up the village to Chapel with Dad, or came back from a concert in the Recreation Room, 'The moon's on his back,' Dad would say. 'It will rain. He carries the water, then tips it out.'

The sights and sounds of home were common yet wonderful. Dad and Mr Bendalls getting a hay seed out of a calf's eye. The shepherd marking his ewes after he had mouthed them to determine their age. 'Mark that un on the rump. Her's lost most of her teeth,' he would say to his assistant. 'Her ull have to go.' Walt Davis as he carried a kerf of hay on his head up the ladder into the tallet for the horses' hay rack.

In the summer-time Mr Carter out late, shirt-sleeved, driving home the ducks off the moat and from the brook. The green eggs he picked up in the morning before he let them out to feed off the wheat in the duck pond.

Mr Carter or Oliver Hampton feeding the ferrets in the row of cages behind the duck pen with a piece of rabbit and bread and milk. The big fitcher ferret Mr Carter kept, like a pole cat. And everywhere men and boys and horses. Waggons, drays, dogs and guns.

Life's little day dawned for me in the sheer magic of the farmyard.

3

The Village Ladder

THE TOP RUNG

Looking back at the 1920s, when I was a boy, it seems to me that there were four rungs to the ladder of village society. The top rung, the men who appeared to make things tick in Ashton, were the farmers and landowners themselves, and a few of the gentry.

The Top Brass

First there was Mr Cambridge who owned and farmed with his younger son a fair slice of the land. An ironmaster from the Black Country, he fell in love with Paris, a hamlet on the hill, as a weekend retreat, years before I was born. Then he bought a lovely black and white house known as The Close. He employed two gardeners, won prizes with roses and daffodils, and when I knew him he travelled first-class to Birmingham after his chauffeur had driven him to the station. He bought land and his son, Howard, farmed it. There was something rather frightening about him we boys felt as he boarded our school train, immaculately dressed and with a king-size cigar. Known as 'The Old Gentleman' he was respected more than anyone in the village.

In his class was old Dr Overthrow, MRCS, who as doctor, Churchwarden, Chairman of the Parish Council and of the School Board, was a powerful figure in the village. He had moved from The Close to Rockland House after his marriage to Amy Bostock, of the aristocratic Bostock family who had been squires here for six hundred years.

Since the death of the last Squire in 1895 the farmland had been divided up into individual farms occupied by working farmers. There was an exception. A John Bostock, a distant relative to the late Squire, continued for a time as a hunting and shooting man and was what would be termed

24

The Close owned by Mr Cambridge, who was often known as 'The Old Gentleman'

today an autocrat. I always touched my cap to him when I saw him walking to Church in his frock coat every Sunday morning.

Our village had not one but two artists living there, both ranked by me among the gentry. George Hughes I found particularly impressive because he had been to school with Lord Birkenhead, but he was friendly and generous to us boys, often travelling on our train home from school with his little leather case and the velour trilby covering his curly, auburn hair (which years later I learnt was a wig). On alighting from the five-past-four train at Ashton, he would slide pennies under our collars so that we could buy bars of Nestlé's chocolate from the slot-machine, and he would always give me sixpence when he came to tea. He lived with his wife at Orchard Cottage and he invited us to his studio there to see his paintings.

In a large Victorian house in Bakers Lane (nicknamed 'Bachelors' Avenue') lived Edward Stidiford, artist and musician, who for some unknown reason was generally known as Tiddley. Many is the hour I have spent with Tiddley sitting in the summer-time on the wooden seat in his front garden. Outside his gate ran one of the many streams of spring water off the hill and the footpath had lots of little stone bridges crossing the stream. The old folks called it the Causeway and spoke of 'walking down the Cause'.

I suppose it is difficult for a man to live alone for seventy-odd years in a village without being considered a little eccentric. I would rather describe Tiddley as interesting. We hear a lot about nature reserves and Tiddley's garden and orchard were just that. He did mow what he called 'the heth' off the thistles and nettles once a year with his scythe, but in the main the birds and the rabbits took over, and the ivy and brambles twined around the moss-covered tree trunks. The apple trees were nondescript, but some of the fruit had a subtle flavour. He gave it to all and sundry, and the flavour of his mellow burgundy pears lingers with me still. If Tiddley had marketed his Nine Square apples or his Russets, I doubt if they would have paid for the picking. He did make a drop of good cider for his older friends, but I was just a boy.

In Tiddley's house his studio with its bay window overlooked the wilderness of his orchard. His pictures of landscapes in oil were considered good by the people who knew, and he had some hung in art exhibitions and

Bakers Lane, often known as Bachelors' Avenue because of the many single men who lived there

26

the second-class galleries. One I remember was of an old apple tree which had fallen over in his orchard, taken root again, and from its horizontal trunk grew fifteen feet vertically and formed a shapely head. He painted it in full bloom with its moss-covered bark. This particular year Tom Bostock had put a bunch of ewes and lambs in the orchard to take advantage of a bit of early keep and Tiddley painted a fine watercolour of the little scene with the Oxford ewe licking her two young lambs under the beautifully natural old tree.

He had a violin which he told me was a Strad; it certainly was a fine instrument, and he played me some beautiful pieces on those summer nights when the wireless was still only paper talk.

When he asked me into his cool, stone-slabbed dining room, I saw a long mahogany table which was covered with drying rose petals, giving off a heavenly perfume. 'Why are all those petals on the table?' I asked.

'Oh tobacco, my boy, is taxed more and more every year. I grow my own, come and see.'

There, on the sunny side of his garden, was one crop tended with care, growing huge leaves of the nicotine plant also ready for drying in his shed. 'You see, my boy, I mix the home grown tobacco with the rose petals and make my smoking mixture.' He lit his pipe and I must say the aroma was pleasing and it must have satisfied him too.

Tiddley's clothes were well worn and threadbare; he kept himself clean but would allow no woman in his house. He was educated at a famous public school which he told me played cricket with the Fosters who caused Worcestershire County Cricket Club to be known as Fostershire. He spoke of W.G. Grace and the great men of cricket.

Tiddley religiously observed one day during the year. It was the Fifth of November. On that night, Tiddley took his muzzle loader gun and shot up into his apple trees to the delight of boys who couldn't afford fireworks. He loaded and reloaded all the evening, the black powder forming a pall of smoke in his little orchard.

The Farmers

At the end of Bakers Lane, named after the second oldest family in the village, stands a large stone house known as The Manor. It used to be called Higford House, but before Mr and Mrs Frank Woods came to live and farm there in the 1920s, the name was changed to make the property sound grander.

Frank was lean and active, with a whimsical smile. His father had been one of the more prosperous market gardeners of Evesham.

Mr and Mrs Woods had their car at about the same time as us. They both drove. It was most unusual to see a lady driving a car in 1925. I saw the produce of Mr Woods' farm pass our house on the way to the station. Alec Barnett was carter, and he came down the hill with a great yellow farm cart stacked high with sprouts or peas according to the season. The thing that struck me about Frank Woods was that he never took half measures over anything. His maxim was that if you plant a couple of acres of peas and the price is high, you don't make a fortune. Of course, if the trade was bad, the loss was small. Frank would plant in a big way and when the returns were high he clicked.

He worked hard and I saw him in his prime on the headland of a pea field talking to Dad. I can still see that mischievous twitch of his nose and the innocent little snigger he uttered as the carter with the pea drill drew the furrows up and down and developed a kink in the rows.

'More peas in a crooked row, Tom,' he'd say to Dad.

Did anyone ever grow such sprouts as Frank Woods did in the Big Ground? I doubt it. Sprouts like coconuts – Byrd Bros. strain – grew one year when cousin Tom picked the equivalent of fourteen nets in thirty-five minutes. In those days they were put in hampers so it was actually seven hampers in thirty-five minutes.

Mrs Maud Woods, a member of a Worcestershire family going back to the Commonwealth, was a particularly good-looking lady. She dressed well and was a good Samaritan to many of the villagers. She and Millie Bostock used to take blancmanges and beef tea to the sick of the parish. Reliable, unassuming, not patronising in any way.

Millie Bostock was a kindly woman; she did a tremendous lot of good. Once Oliver was down with lumbago. He wouldn't have the doctor so Millie, who was a very amateur nurse, having once worked in a doctor's house, put some sort of plaster on his back which fetched quite a bit of skin off and Oliver was not at all pleased. Millie boasted she had more bones in the churchyard than anyone in the village. She lived in one of our cottages and we looked forward to her coming over to pay her rent, which took the whole evening. She was a spinster of sixty plus. We heard about her love affairs; how she nearly married the captain of Evesham Fire Brigade, then a music master from Stratford-upon-Avon. She said, 'All young men should have a spell in the army to straighten their backs.' She was a keen gardener; she also ran the Mother's Union. Millie was a practical Christian in every way.

David Dunn was a small farmer, and although the Vicar told him that it's not good for a man to live alone, he remained single. Besides his farm, he did hauling for the Council – stone off Holcombe Nap for the roads. He kept ten heavy Shire horses and, before the new line was made from Honeybourne Junction to Cheltenham, David hauled all the necessities of life with his heavy drays from Beckford station on our branch line to points way up on the Cotswolds. Walt Davis was his head carter for some years. They started early in the morning with a horse and dray, and, if the road to travel was a hilly one, they took a trace horse besides. Walt said to me: 'My boy, that was a job, getting ten osses in at five in the morning. I had to catch um all, mind, by Shaw Green, halfway up the hill, then tail um together tandem fashion an bring um down to Bachelors' Avenue and into the stable. Then mind,' he continued, 'I had to fill their nosebags with fittle corn chaff and hang these on the back axle of the drays. Ten o'clock some nights when the last dray came whome. I udn't do it agin mind, better to be in quod.' Walt described David as the biggest hypocrite that ever lived. 'Chapel bloke,' he added. 'No Saturday arternoons off and fifteen bob a week.' When I knew David, he had mellowed with age. He still used two strawberry roan Shires to pull the water carts when our village street was done in the macadam style.

The primrose and the violet coppice were a part of David's estate. Here lay some of David's wealth, for the whole area – a boggy hollow at one end and a mossy bank at the other – grew timber. In fact, it would be misleading to call it timber, it was a withy bed, or a sally bed, in the moister parts and an ash coppice on the drier bank.

The withies grew on stools (short stumps) and were cut as osiers – bundles like boltings of straw – and sold to the Evesham hamper makers to make containers for market produce. Withies, gleaming and golden, were to be seen standing in their tidy bundles in the stream which skirted the coppice and flowed down Bachelors' Avenue. This was to prevent them from drying out and to keep them supple. The smaller osiers tied up the bundles of a hundred and twenty buds of asparagus and the dozen bunches of spring onions ready for the market.

The sally or sallow stools grew poles suitable for ladder rungs. In the early spring, David's sally was a pleasing sight as the pussy willow buds changed colour almost daily. First a greenish grey and finally, as the buds turned to full bloom, the lemon yellow of the pollen became alive with bees.

Master Dunn, as some of my friends referred to David, had several hilly pastures for his horses. The Leasows, Heets Hill, Canks Bank. 'Thistles,' Walt said. 'We wanted a feow donkeys up there to ut um off.'

Jasper Hill spliting withies for use as fencing

David was the last of a long line of yeoman farmers. He wasn't a bad sort really but these old horsey types did appear to treat their horses rather better than their men.

John Bostock's sons followed various occupations. Jack was a market gardener at Paris. He grew cherries and daffodils. Tom farmed The Croft, a little holding of fruit where he kept a few cows and pigs and made hay with Bill Allen (known as Blenheim) in the Languet, a hill field. 'I pick the fruit when it's mella,' he told me (in other words 'ripe').

Tom was a jovial type. He was called Laughing Tom because he laughed at everything. No one quite knew whether he was obliged to work or not. It was come day, go day, God sent Sunday. He made some of the most potent cider the village has ever tasted. He was also a pig-killer, and all the time he killed, cleaned and cut up the pig, we would be entertained with his flow of interesting anecdotes and practical advice on how to salt bacon. 'Now every thing is fit to eat in the pig,' he would say, 'bar the squeal. There's as many ways of cutting a pig up as there is pigs. Dost want much mate out on him or dost want it left on the flitch?' Then he would tell us a tale about one he killed for Harry Stallard the baker. It was as thin as a hurdle and Harry wanted plenty of griskin and spare ribs taken out and, laughing enough to choke, Tom said, 'I'll be dalled if you couldn't see through the flitches. Talk about streaky bacon. It ut a-made hoss whips.'

Will was an authority on local history. He collected rates and did people's income tax accounts, that is to say, those few people who paid tax. He had a game leg and cycled round with a walking stick strapped on the cross-bar so that, when he had to walk, he could do so without too much trouble. He succeeded the doctor as Chairman of the Parish Council and knew every footpath and bridleway in the village; Will was a mine of information as he slowly deliberated his opinion, which was so often right.

Jack, Tom and Will were among the last of the true yeomen who fattened their pigs and bred game-cocks for roasting; their sister Kate churned the butter and scrubbed the white kitchen table. These men and women cherished their independence but always helped the less fortunate.

THE SECOND RUNG

The second rung of the village ladder, as I saw it, held the men and women who formed the 'middle class' of the village. The shopkeepers, the blacksmith, the porter-in-charge at the railway station.

The Shopkeepers

Mr and Mrs Stallard kept the Post Office and Stores, and they also had a Bake House. I often stood with Frank and watched Mr Stallard sweating at the bake oven door handling the wooden peel like the oar of a boat and using it shovel-like to bring the excellent bread out of the oven. Batch cakes, cottage loaves, the long since forgotten four-pound loaf, dough cakes. To recapture the smell of fresh-baked bread of that age is to bring back in memory days of sunshine from early morning till late at night, of the lightly-sprung baker's cart waiting with scrubbed shelves to receive the unadvertised product of stone-ground flour and yeast, of the tempting crust which no boy could resist sampling from the batch cakes. An impatient cob called Express daily drew the cart to the Bredon Hill villages. No thermometer told Mr Stallard or the other local bakers how hot to get their ovens; it was just an inborn instinct like a country woman sticking a knife in her cake to see if it was done. The bakers of bread were master men; they baked dough cakes and cooked Christmas dinners for families in their big ovens and dried home-cured bacon in their chimneys, but bread was their main concern. With potatoes, bread was the staple diet for the Ashton men who worked on the land.

Mr Stallard also milked cows and his forty ewes and the ram grazed around the beeches of the Cuckoo Pen while his store cattle lay on Holcombe Nap. His family delivered the milk, Mr Stallard's eggs were graded into several baskets and Mrs Stallard made superb butter. And so back in about 1925 Mr Stallard, with his dray, laden with lambs or a calf, pulled by a bit of good horseflesh, was a familiar sight down our village street on market days, on his way to Evesham, Beckford or Tewkesbury.

A genial man was Mr Stallard, like Dad and Mr Carter. Quick on the trigger at the running rabbit. A keen follower of football and cricket and, most important to me, he liked boys. He seemed to understand us.

He often told me of the Club feasts in his father's yard. The outdoor quoits in the garden of the pub. He had probably forgotten more about the making of good cider than most people ever knew. Then he grew osiers down in the withy bed for making hampers. There was in Ashton at that time a number of men who bought and sold orchards of fruit, mainly apples, Mr Stallard was one of them.

Mr Tandy and his wife took over the Post Office from the Stallards, and although they stocked the basic commodities from boiled sweets to Carter's seeds, the villagers came to them mostly for postage stamps and their 'Lloyd George' (as they called the pension). It was the village shop, run by

The lightly-sprung baker's cart ready to make deliveries to the Bredon Hill villages

The village shop in Ashton, run by Mrs Collins, which provided for many of the villagers' needs

Mrs Collins, which provided most of the villagers' needs, from paraffin to custard powder. Behind the counter, where a simple bacon slicer would cut bacon of a more reasonable thickness than the modern machines, Mrs Collins stood surrounded by all the groceries, the candles, the cigarettes and tobacco.

On hot days in the summer she turned the handle on her old ice-making machine to make yellow ice-cream at a halfpenny a cone. Word quickly went round the village school, and the children would crowd into her shop clutching their halfpennies.

The little window lit by a flickering oil lamp would be tastefully dressed for Christmas with white mesh Christmas stockings, pink sugar mice, and an almost life-size dummy of Santa Claus peeping through the window.

The Midnight Milkman

The doctor's eldest son was always known as Buckram. Like his father, he was an excellent shot. His father lived until Buckram was twenty-six years old, but the doctor was an old man and with his practice and his other commitments he took little interest in guiding Buckram or his younger brother into the professions, business or the art of farming the land. As a youth Buckram took charge of the family farm. He bought a small herd of North Devon heifers and at twenty years of age, when the heifers produced crossbred Hereford calves by our bull, Buckram began his career as a dairyman.

With his churn on a milk float and Bob between the shafts, Buckram soon became a feature of village life, carrying the milk bucket with a pint and quart measure slung on its brass looped handle, selling milk to the villagers.

The Overthrow custom of late rising was carried on by Buckram. He was late all day, every day. He became known as the 'Midnight Milkman'. Buckram had a deep bass singing voice, and I have often heard him singing those old harvest hymns at the midnight hour, 'All is safely gathered in, free from sorrow free from sin', accompanied by the clanking milk pail and the sound of Bob grazing the roadside verge.

The empty jugs were put out on the cottage door-steps at bedtime. When the landworkers rose at dawn, the pints and quarts of milk were there, covered by blue slates as a protection from the night's prowling cats. Saturdays were the exception, when Buckram milked his cows early and delivered to his customers before tea-time. In smart Norfolk jacket, lovat breeches, polished boots and leggings, Buckram would be bound for

Buckram Overthrow, the 'Midnight Milkman'

Cheltenham in the brass-radiatored motor car he had bought to chauffeur the doctor around.

Unshaven in the week with his everlasting Woodbine and his dung-caked trousers, Buckram was transformed on Saturdays, with Brylcreemed hair and a cigar. Sacco, his friend the mason, dressed in blazer and flannels with a gaudy bow tie, rode beside him in the two-seater with wooden spoked wheels and shining brass headlamps. Sometimes they went to the Opera House, and other times to the Daffodil Cinema, and then on to a well-known pub, a haunt of pedlars, street traders and dealers. More than once I've seen this flaxen-haired farmer with a painted lady in the gardens of Rockland House.

The farm had been split by the coming of the railway in 1864. New Piece, an arable field, was on the village side of the line, while the pastures were on the other. In New Piece, Buckram grew mangolds for the cows and some oats. He was no arable farmer, always ploughing late, planting late and harvesting late. I well remember him coming to the yard to borrow our Ransome horse plough. He returned it in pieces, the body separate from the tails and the wheels. Mr Carter, Dad's partner, was there when he brought it back and I remember the look on his face. 'What the nation have you done to our plough,' he spluttered.

The cowshed housed the four cows (there was room for no more than six). A room at the end of the shed served as a dairy, if one could call it a dairy, and there he kept cattle-cake and various items of harness. Outside, the hayrick stood under the hedge. The cows drank from a pond where tadpoles turned to frogs every summer. The milk was poured directly from his bucket into a churn and was delivered warm from the cows. Unhygienic you may say, but the winner at the local baby show was fed on Buckram's milk.

Two other milkmen delivered in the village, but, despite their tidy brass churns and their shining stainless steel buckets, Buckram survived. The old folk remained loyal to the Midnight Milkman. My Uncle George and Aunt Annie had Buckram's milk, and I well remember one Sunday night when their milk was delivered on the doorstep at one o'clock in the morning.

'Is this morning or evening delivery?' Uncle called from his bedroom window. Buckram's heavy boots clattered down the stone path from the cottage while Uncle heard in the still air of the early morning, 'We plough the fields and scatter the good seed on the land.'

*. . . on a bare patch in our rickyard where the grass had been killed
by the scratching over the years of our hundred or so fowls, we fed
them twice a day, . . .*

*Saturday mornings I usually took one or two horses to the
blacksmiths in Baker's Lane to have them reshod.*

The Company Man

Our porter-in-charge (we couldn't run to a gold-braided 'Station Boss', as they were known in the village) was not an easy man for boy-chaps to please. He was a sandy-moustached, lean fellow who worked in the station in shifts with an under-porter. He was the sort of man who had two natures; his booking office manner when he issued tickets to all stations to Birmingham, or Ashchurch, could be quite charming, especially to the few first-class passengers who travelled on the line. But out in the siding when a truck of 'artificial' came in or when he was helping load sprouts, apples and all the riches of our village for the industrial north, we will say he was 'unco-operative'. Jim found this out when he first started taking our milk to the station. Seventeen gallons of milk plus the churn weighs something approaching two hundredweight and Jim was only a boy-chap. The eight-ten to Ashchurch left Platform Two on the other side of the line. Jim usually arrived in good time and pulled the little four-wheeled trolley, with Midland Railway painted on the side, close up to his dray or float, and waited for Wilf the porter-in-charge to come out of the station house and

Ashton Station run by Wilf, the porter-in-charge

help him to load four or five churns on to the railway trolley ready to be pulled across the level crossing and, with an extra push, up on to the opposite platform. Just as the front of the little tank engine, with four coaches, emerged from underneath the road bridge, Wilf shot through the little white garden gate and made for Jim. The churns were manoeuvred with difficulty on to the trolley, Jim doing his best and Wilf swearing his best. Meanwhile the guard was getting impatient and the engine driver had to reverse the train to let Wilf and Jim cross the level crossing with their load. This happened most mornings and young Jim's elder brother told him, 'If old Wilf keeps on swearing at you, ask him for a form so that you can report him to Derby.'

Next morning Wilf gave Jim his usual mouthful and, although a little nervous, Jim plucked up courage and said, 'I've had enough of your language every morning. Give me a form to fill in and I'll report ya to Derby.' Wilf ran into the booking hall, his moustache bristling as he used every swear word and oath he knew and some that Jim had not heard before. In a mad passion he opened one drawer after the other, throwing forms in all directions.

'Report me to Derby, you little snot, I'll report you to your gaffers.'

Jim said George Bendalls wanted another consignment book. This upset him still more. 'You chaps uses our consignment books for toilet paper, you only had one the other day.'

Jim had many more battles with Wilf but never again did he threaten to report him to Derby.

Cold winter evenings when Jim had sprouts to load for all points north, Wilf took a lot of coaxing out of his snug booking office. 'Go and get the truck lid down, it's the fifth one along for Nottingham, I'll be there in a minute.' Young Jim had often unloaded his half ton and struggled to fasten the truck lid before Wilf ambled along the siding, blowing his hands and with half a Woodbine hanging from under his moustache. 'Some empty churns on the platform,' Wilf would say and he did help young Jim on to the dray with them. Sometimes a churn of milk came back sour; we had to pay the carriage on it and Wilf's pig, which he kept in an old railway carriage under the pear tree, had sour milk with his barley meal for a few days.

Most Ashtonians called the Midland Railway 'The Company'. Wilf with his tidy station and his smart uniform was strictly a 'Company man'. He carried on working during the General Strike in 1926.

The Cobbler

In a Georgian brick-built house with its windows darkened by an over-grown yew tree lived John Clopton the 'snob' (the cobbler). The house was roomy; it belonged to Mr Bostock, together with a large garden and a row of pigsties. John never married and lived with his sister and brother-in-law Old Man Hyde, who made shoes to measure for some of the gentry. John had picked up a certain amount of Mr Hyde's art after he had done his time in the Army, being pensioned off as a sergeant-major.

Just to see John's military bearing was sufficient to impress anyone that he was no ordinary tiller of the soil. True, he did keep a few pigs and a good vegetable garden, and when old Mr Hyde got past mending the shoes of the villagers, John mended shoes for whom he pleased. His Army pension gave him independence. In fact, when he mended shoes for anyone he left him in no doubt that it was a favour.

The easiest way to rile John was to take him a pair of shoes which had been mended by someone else before. A local gentleman had several fine pairs of riding boots, and his little servant girl, Elsie, took a pair to be soled and heeled by John. John had a trimmed military moustache, tobacco stained, and he wore pince-nez spectacles which he peered over when he spoke, all rather frightening for a young girl. The boots had been repaired before elsewhere and John could see this at a glance. He threw them back at little Elsie shouting, 'Take them to the man who repaired them last time.'

Elsie whispered, 'They belong to a friend of Master Bostock.'

This infuriated John still more and opening his workshop door he replied, 'Get out, girl, and the boots, I don't care if they belong to the King of England.'

'Passionate,' Tom Wheatcroft called him. 'That unt all as he's passionate with either,' Tom said. 'He cuts the sticks and gets the coal in for Ray Lewes' widda.' Tom's eyes had that wicked glint in them and I knew when Tom added, 'Oi thur's more to it than that,' that John and Mrs Lewes were possibly a little more than friends. 'And what about Mildred at the bottom of the village?' Tom cleared his throat. 'Thur's temptation if you like.'

I said, 'John feeds her pigs.'

'Oi, I know,' Tom said, 'but they dropped out the other day – John and Mildred. You see, John unt at the top of Mildred's list. Master Bostock with the gammy leg have put John's nose out lately, and the other morning when I took the cows back from milking past that drooping ash by Mildred's, she was at the bedroom window. I didn't ketch all as was said between um but I did hear John tell her. "Mildred, I hate you and if I had a gun I'd shoot you." I udn't put it past him neither,' and as Tom said this there was a sort of a smile come over his face as much as to say 'good riddance to bad rubbish'.

Tom summed up by telling me, 'Thur's two sorts a passion and bwoth of um wants taking in moderation. Mind tha, John learnt a smart bit out in India.'

A neighbour of mine, a youth in his teens, ploughboy for Mr Cambridge, took his hobnailed boots to John, worn down to the uppers. John swore at him, ran him round the workshop with a horse whip and promised to tell the youth's father about him letting his boots get in such a state. Swearing was probably one of John's worst points.

The landlord of the Plough and Harrow, prompted by the vicar who was worried about the effect on the village lads of John Clopton's language, installed a swear box in the bar. The language generally improved and a few odd coppers were all that went into the swear box. There was, of course, the one exception, John Clopton. The very thought of a swear box started John swearing. One night John made one of his irregular visits to the pub. he had just drawn his Army pension. 'Moderate your language, John,' the landlord told him as he entered the bar. 'Or else most of your pension will go to charity in the swear box.'

John Clopton started swearing, using every word he could think of, and kept up a constant stream for an hour, all the time putting his pennies in the box. He drank beer at others' expense and his fellow drinkers changed his money into coppers just to listen to John's terrible curses. By closing time he had repeated over and over again every word in the book. A short while after, he died from a heart attack and I watched his coffin pass our house on the bier covered in the Union Jack. Years later men still recalled that night at the Plough and Harrow.

THE THIRD RUNG

It would be wrong to assume that all the farm workers were of the same status. The shepherd, the carter, the cowman were specialists. They knew all about the rearing and care of farm animals, and were responsible for them seven days a week, the sheep, the working horses and the cattle. They made decisions on the best time to dip or shear the sheep, when to plough or to mow, when to wean the calves. With the self-employed and the smallholders, they were on the third rung of the village ladder.

With the other boys of the village, I mingled, grey-jerseyed with the corduroyed shepherds, cowmen and carters. There were always these staid men around, standing, leaning, often bent, but corner-stones. Men who gave a sense of eternity to an unexplained world.

As a child it was always plain to me that The Masters, as they were known, rarely gave orders to the three key men on the farm. The conversation went like this. 'Well, Walt, do you think the duckfoot drags will rise enough mould for the Telegraph peas, or the Larkworthy scuffle?'

Walt's eyebrows would rise as he answered, 'You be men as pays, but if I was you I ud keep the scuffle off the ploughing. It ull only bring the nasty wet clay on top. The ducksfoot ull make a clinking job with three osses abreast.'

The Old Shepherd

The old shepherd was very close to the soil and to all living things except his fellow men. He only mixed at busy times, otherwise his life was lonely. It was considered an honour to help him at his work. There was something very stable about him and he seemed to have an inner peace and serenity. He was more or less his own boss over the sheep and his word was taken as law both by the other workers and usually by his employers.

A man born and bred on the Cotswolds, he seemed more at home on Bredon Hill than in the Vale. He worked according to the weather and the season. No need to tell him how to spend a wet day on the land. He would be found in the granary, stripped to his shirt sleeves, turning the wheel on the cake grinder. The kibbled linseed and cotton-seed oil cake flowed in a constant stream into the bushel measure as one slab after another was fed into the kibbler. 'Thur unt the goodness in this cake like thur used to be, Fred lad,' he said. 'They crushes it too hard and squeezes all the oil out on it.'

Bronchitis never stopped the shepherd. He worked, he joked and the scent of his twist tobacco smoke as it swirled in blue eddies around the beams was just one of the little pleasures of his life.

When I read about Moses and the Prophets I thought of the shepherd and imagined them to be men like him. To be in his company was my ambition on holiday from school. He dressed for his job among sheep. His cord trousers were known as fall-fronted or broad falls, fastened up the sides like breeches with buttons. We called them tailboard front. He wore a corduroy waistcoat with lots of pockets, one for his watch, an old turnip watch, almost as big as a small clock. His thick silver watch chain had a golden sovereign on it. One pocket was for his tobacco tin. In another

Shepherd Corbisley with his dog, Rosie

would be a tin of Stockholm tar and some raddle. His coat – when he wore it – was of dark grey fustian, a hard-wearing cloth of heavy weft. I never saw him in anything else but an Oxford shirt with a blue stripe in it. Just below his knees he wore some leather straps called yorks. When I asked him what they were for he said, 'Oi, to kip the dust out of me eyes.' But I found out that their main purpose was to give the trousers a little fullness at the knee, and when he was sweating in the summertime and his clothes stuck to his body this would prevent his broad leather braces pulling the buttons off his trousers. At lambing-time he wore something like a pinafore frock made of hurden or sacking tied with binder twine around his waist. When he wasn't smoking it, he stuck his clay pipe under the band of his battered trilby; and his crook and well-dubbined hobnail boots completed his working outfit. On the occasional Sunday when he found time to come to chapel I thought he looked a little like the Aga Khan; his features were distinguished.

On entering the Cross Barn lambing pen or the granary you could smell on him a mixture of Jeyes fluid used to kill sheep maggots, or Stockholm tar for healing wounds, twist tobacco, cider and sheep. Not that he wasn't clean. Mrs Corbisley's washing was whiter than the driven snow that the shepherd sometimes had to dig his ewes out of on Bredon.

At lambing-time he left his dog with Mrs Corbisley at night and I have been with him coming away from his house when he said to his dog Rosie, 'Now look arter her, mind.'

One year our ewes had liver fluke very badly and many died. The shepherd said to me, 'When they have got a lump under thur jaw and goes glassy-eyed it's soon all over.' The shepherd got very upset about losing so many ewes. He talked of jumping in the moat when he fetched his money one Friday night. Dad said, 'We're not blaming you. It's bad all over the country.' The shepherd added that he didn't mind carrying any tool about with him, however heavy, 'but not this yer spade.'

When the lambs were big enough, the wind was in the right direction, and the shepherd had a convenient day, they had to have their tails cut and the male lambs were castrated. This was done in the Cross Barn. He used a bone-handled knife, as old as himself and very sharp, to cut the lambs' tails. The ram lambs were held by Bert Wheatcroft by all four legs, the lamb resting against Bert's chest. The shepherd cut off the purse, then he leaned forward, drew the stones out with the few teeth he had left, and dropped them in a bucket. All the time he chewed twist tobacco and spat in the wound he made in each ram lamb. The shepherd's whiskers and moustache were stained with twist tobacco and blood; the ewe lambs didn't bother much, running off minus their tails, but the ram lambs, suffering from shock, sometimes lay still for a few seconds before rushing out of the back door of the barn. The tails and sweetbreads were cooked by Mrs Corbisley and it's possible that the butcher didn't have to call that week.

He generally left about twenty or so of the late lambs until they got a bit bigger. On Friday night in our courtyard when he fetched his money Dad would say 'Shepherd, don't you think you ought to cut those other few lambs Monday?'

'They beunt hardly big enough, Master. Give um another wick.' We all knew that by that time the old shepherd would have a better meal from them, but who could blame him?

On Saturday afternoons the shepherd would be in his garden by his potato and beetroot bury with a pair of steel-rimmed glasses perched at the end of his nose, while several villagers waited with wicker baskets holding young tom-cats. He looked quite a professional man as he performed this delicate operation.

At haymaking time, the shepherd would be asked if he could help in the hayfields, and with building the rick. Getting the old man down the ladder once the rick was built was quite a job. As he put his trembling hand on the top rung, Dad, who was on the rick with him, held his other arm, while another man stood on the bottom round of the forty-round ladder; then one foot at a time the shepherd descended. When he reached the ground he said, 'Thur, I udn't go up on that rick again for five pounds.'

He built the straw rick thatching and one year, as I moved the boltings to him, he said, 'This straw unt do for thatching. It's knocked about too much with these new machines. Thur was nothing like the 'ooden drum to turn out a straight bolting.' The machine we were using was about thirty years old but the shepherd was a diehard.

The Carter

Walt, our carter, had eight working horses, two nags and an old pony to look after when I first knew him. He lived up at Paris, a little hamlet on the hill, and he carried his coal, paraffin, bread, in fact everything, up through the young orchard of Bramley apples, then on across Boss Close, up the narrow path to his cottage. I never saw Walt go home from work without having something to carry. 'I s'pose I shall 'a to hump this half-hundred-weight of coal up tonight,' he remarked as he got his back under the bag that David Dunn had left for him on the wall by the thatched cart house. So with either a Woodbine or a pipe of Red Bell and his back bent he made for home, a half mile tramp saying, 'Shan't be sorry to have a cup of tay.'

Walt fetched his water from the spring, had no modern sanitation, grew his own potatoes, fetched his horses in at five o'clock in the morning and worked until dark, haymaking and harvest.

He treated his ploughboys fairly although he had a hard upbringing himself. As a boy he worked for a farmer who treated him hard, made him sleep in an attic and didn't allow him a candle for fear of fire. Breakfast was of cider sop (bread soaked in cider), and the carter he worked under thought nothing of giving him a stroke or two with the horse whip.

Walt had a wonderful assortment of boots in the harness room near the stable. Some had pieces cut out of them to ease his corns and bunions. He packed his boots with wool and toe rags. No doubt his feet were painful and after ploughing some nights, as we sat on the bench in the harness room while the horses munched at their chopped bait of chaff, mangolds and oat flour, old Walt would say, 'My fit be that sore, they be just like liver. Ast got ere a Woodbine? I ant got one, nor a wift a 'bacca.' I kept a few for him (and had an occasional one myself) and fetched his Red Bell tobacco, threepence halfpenny for half an ounce, from the village shop.

Walt the carter with one of his favourite horses

Walt was usually last to fetch his money from our courtyard window on a Friday night when Dad would be seated at the big table in the hall as the pay envelopes disappeared one by one. Walt would say 'Well, Master, ant that ploughing gone bad! I've never had a job like that afore. Stick, moot, clog, no slip to it,' and rubbing his bare arms, he added 'and ant that gen my arms summat. Another day or two like this un and I'll be on the box.' Dad would say, 'When do you think you will finish the job, Walt?' 'Finish it! It won't be next wick. And what about some corn for my 'osses? Master Carter won't let me start the clover rick and they'll soon be as thin as hurdles.' Dad would reply, 'I'll see Mr Carter starts a cut on the clover rick but be careful. Mind, it's a long while till May Day.'

Walt mowing with his favourite pair, the brothers Boxer and Turpin, made a fine sight. Turpin was a liver chestnut with massive shoulders. We hadn't got a collar big enough for him and the Beckford saddler came up and measured him for a new one. Boxer, a true chestnut, about sixteen hands compared with Turpin's seventeen, was Walt's spoilt child. When the bree flies and 'old maids' (horse flies) were 'laying holt', as Walt put it, these horses, swishing their tails, took Walt round the field at almost a jog trot. The view from the front was a mass of elderberry blossom laced around the horses' 'mullins' to keep some of the flies from around their eyes, ears and noses. Every time Walt got off his machine to oil up he smacked the horses' briskets with his hands, killing these bloodsuckers and the bree flies which laid their eggs on the feather part of the leg about the hocks. Sometimes the 'old maids' sampled the blood from Walt's arms which were bare to his elbows.

'Tell yer father that fust ground I cut wants moving with the swath turner. We'm a gwain to get a rattle afore long.' I knew he meant thunder and as he spke a whirly wind took some of the partly-made hay up into the air almost out of sight.

He started his mowing early, often at first light; and when the midday sun was pouring down, the horses were rested in the shade while Walt went hay pitching; then he went on mowing in the cool of the evening. His frail at haymaking, which he hung on the horse's hames as he left the stable and then put in some shady spot for bait time, was both a food basket and a tool bag. Besides his food and drink, he carried an oil can, a screw spanner, shut links, mowing-machine blade sections, a file, a punch and a hammer. He carried out all small repairs in the field, but if there was anything more serious he'd say, 'Fred, gu down to Segebrra and fetch young Tom Harris.' Tom was the blacksmith and came on a motor-bike with box sidecar. Although Walt called him young, he must have been

Mowing the hay on a hot afternoon

knocking on for seventy, but Walt knew his father and Tom would always be young Tom.

Walt was a wit and at the last Harvest Supper, a joint affair with Beckford, Fred Pickford asked if anybody wanted any more food. The men having had just about as much as they could manage, Walt said, 'Yes, gaffer. I do.' A hush went over the gathering and Walt waited a few seconds before he added, 'Tomorrow night.' He could sing a song himself and I loved to hear him at the village concerts sing,

> 'I love the green fields
> And I love the sunshine,
> The robin with pretty red breast;
> I love pussy cat
> Fast asleep on the mat,
> But I love my dear mother the best.'

'Life's allus bin the same, ever since Adam was a boy,' was his favourite saying.

The Cowman

In 1924, we had an outbreak of foot-and-mouth at Stanley Farm. This was a grim time for everyone, but it was especially bad for George Bendalls, the cowman.

George had experienced setbacks in the past; we once lost a cow with anthrax; the occasional one developed garget or mastitis for which, in those days before antibiotics were available, little could be done; a calf would die of the dreaded white scour and Joker the bull frequently got loose at night. But this was different.

George had reared most of the seventeen cows from calves and he knew them all by name and they knew him.

Just before the first cow was shot in our back garden, George came to our window with tears making little rivulets down his sun-tanned old face, trickling down through the grey stubble – some dripping from his chin and others from the end of his pointed nose. Seeing George crying shook me, a small boy still at Prep school. 'Master Archer,' he began, 'I can't stop here and see this lot, do you think I could go home?'

Dad said, 'We'll manage, George, you go home. I understand.'

I can still smell the stench of the huge funeral pyre which burnt the carcasses all that night, and carried on burning for a week.

As the years at Prep school passed and George Bendalls' health failed, Tom Wheatcroft became cowman for Mr Carter and Dad. We were rearing calves and not milking when Tom came.

For a year or two I was a sort of understudy to him but almost lived with him at work during school holidays. I became particularly attached to him because he worked a lot of his time around the buildings of Stanley Farm. Here he foddered the winter-yarded cattle and suckled the calves, three on each cow, in the long shed. I well remember sitting on the manger edge with him while the white-faced, dark red calves sucked and bunted the patient Shorthorn cows.

Tom carried a little nut stick and when a cow kicked at a newly bought calf of a week or so old he would say, 'Now then, old girl, stand still, ull ya?' The cow would rattle the tie chain, turn and show the whites of her eyes, half-expecting a stroke from Tom's stick.

'Tis all done by kindness,' he said to me.

After he had suckled the calves and fed and watered the cows and store cattle in winter, there were about forty-strong store cattle wintering on the top of Bredon, and after ten o'clock bait I went up there with him to help him 'fother' them, as he said. We kept Turpin, a dependable horse, up

The cowman with Joker the bull. Mr Harry Carter, Tom Archer's partner, is standing by the cow crib

there for the winter, a set of fillers gears and a muck-cart to cart the hay to the forty stores, which were also having cake, ready for Gloucester market about April time. We called at Paris, the small hamlet two grounds away from our village, and Tom popped in a little cottage there to see if his aged mother was all right.

Tom split withy sticks on wet days and made rick pegs for thatching the hayricks. I suppose the day men worked long hours too, but they did get their weekends off.

Tom Wheatcroft was a cow doctor. Vets were first employed by the Army and it is not so long ago that they only attended horses. Tom had remedies galore; if a cow lost its cud or was unable to bring back its food to ruminate, Tom had a remedy. He drenched it with an evil-smelling mixture. When I say he drenched it, I mean he poured the liquid down its throat with a pint-and-a-half bottle filled over and over again. Drench seems to be the operative word. First of all he boiled a large saucepan full of cabbage and fat bacon which had gone rancid, or 'reasty' as we called it. This was boiled until all the goodness had come out of the cabbage, leaving a green liquid, and the fat from the bacon left a scale of oily substance, a kind of scum on the top. After straining through a colander, the medicine was allowed to cool to blood heat. Next came the drenching. Can you imagine anything more likely to bring back food than this mixture of boiled bacon and cabbage water?

Badger lost condition after her fourth calf and was tied up in the long shed, looking very sorry for herself. She had developed a cough, was scouring badly, and refusing the most tempting food Tom offered her. The official vet arrived, an Irishman who was very down to earth. He examined the cow which was making a roaring noise as she breathed. Dad came along and said to Mr Macquire that he wondered if a piece of mangold had got stuck in her gullet. Tom spoke up, 'No, Master, if it was that her ud be swelled up round the brisket.'

Mr Macquire put his his hand on Tom's shoulder and said, 'You have a good man here, Mr Archer. He's quite right. I know of men who have taken their degree at Edinburgh University who would not have noticed that. It's TB. Send for the knacker.'

The Rough Carpenter

Oliver Hampton was to be reckoned among the specialists. He was the most ingenious man I have ever known. He worked for Dad and Mr Carter as their rough carpenter. A bachelor, he lived in a little thatched cottage known as the Cross, lodging with my Aunt Phoebe. Oliver had turned an old tumbledown barn near the cottage into a workshop.

Oliver was a little bent man and he needed to be. The roof was as low as if it was built to fit him. Many a pleasant summer evening I have spent in there, sitting on Oliver's chopping block and watching him make or mend some old tool or other. From wooden pegs sticking out from the wall hung ladders of all lengths. As well as ladders in Oliver's place were pieces of wood in various stages of seasoning; larch poles for ladder-making, red withy for ladder rounds (rungs), ash for axe helves, shuppick stales and rabbit-wire pegs. There were piles of wood shavings, sawdust, gate hooks, and other apparent junk, all useful for something. His tools cut like razors and as he sharpened them with his whetstones of different kinds, all the time he chewed twist tobacco, which became evident as he moistened the various whetstones with spittle.

Oliver's talents were varied but I think he liked working in wood the best. He mended our gates, put shafts on waggons, horse rolls, did a bit of bricklaying, and was an expert in the dying art of dry-stone walling.

About July every year his evenings were spent making pegs to hold rabbit

A stick of rabbits caught on Bredon Hill

wires from cleft ash, dry and seasoned. They were driven into the ground with a mallet made by Oliver from crab-apple wood with an ash handle. The oval-shaped snares which Oliver set in the rabbit runs were propped about two inches off the ground by a small nut stick with a groove in the top, cut from the nut bushes alongside the path to our privy.

The rabbits on Bredon were strong and weighty and often broke the factory-made wires which were woven from six strands of plain brass wire. Oliver made his own. Suspended from a beam in his workshop he hung eight strands of wire, and with a lead weight at the bottom, he spun this round to make his wires threading the one end through a small eye he fixed in the other. 'They won't wear them necklaces until I faked um a bit,' he told me. This he did by making a fire of wood shavings and smoking the wires until the shiny newness had gone.

His ladders were all hand-made. His sixty-rung was for walnut picking and roof repairs, and his forty-rung for picking the Pitmaston Duchess pears in the Cross Barn orchard or for putting bolt upright against the end of a hayrick. He made unusual ladders with a slight curve, about fifteen rungs, so that the man unloading a load of hay or corn could get on the waggon and, once he was up there, give the ladder a push to fall on the ground out of the way. The slight curve, or cant, as Oliver called it, saved it from breaking as it fell like a boomerang. Short ladders he made for cottagers to hang their pig carcasses on, to await cutting-up next day. He once made a short ladder for blackberrying, about eight rounds long, so that his niece could reach the best berries on top of the hedges.

From October until early March every year Oliver's main job was rabbiting. He and Mr Carter set the wires and I followed behind with the mallet driving in the pegs. They both set these snares almost as fast as they could walk and we usually kept in a straight line across the fields so that they could be found at night.

With a carbide cycle lamp I went up Bredon with Oliver and Mr Carter in the dark winter's evenings to look around the wires. Now old Oliver, who probably knew more about the lie of the land this side of the hill than anyone, took short, quick steps, and with his head well forward set the pace as we made for the first lot of wires. Here and there a snared rabbit could be seen in the light of the lamp, sometimes sitting quite still, to be quickly killed by Oliver or Mr Carter dislocating its neck, the next perhaps already dead, the sudden stop as its head went in the snare breaking the neck at once.

Have you ever been in someone's company and felt absolutely safe from all harm? That feeling came over me as I walked with these men of staid nature and vast experience. Some of Oliver's conversation with Mr Carter will stick for ever in my memory, also their mannerisms and parochial outlook. This was the late twenties and early thirties. Millions were unemployed and as Oliver told his tales without thought of the Depression he always ended with, 'That's the truth, the certain truth and the truth needs no study.'

They talked of births and deaths in the village. Mr Carter mentioned that another Bradfield had been born and Oliver said, 'Oi, they carries these parcels about so long then they drops um.' Then Mr Carter continued more seriously to talk of the text at Chapel the last Sunday. 'I suppose, Oliver, that we're both on trespass down here. We're only promised three-score years and ten.'

The Smallholders

Farms and estates are not exactly what one sees on picture postcards, there are always the awkward lands, the smaller farms which lie farthest from the village, the farms with rambling, cold houses where life is a constant struggle, coping with stock where the buildings are poor and the water supply dependent on the weather, and the distant fields usually in bad heart, neglected by the muck-cart owing to the distance from the cattle yard. These outlying farms were let to tenant farmers, men who had just put their foot on the next round of the ladder, men who had saved a few pounds after being labourers, which enabled them to pay the moderate rent asked for these difficult holdings.

These men had started on their upward struggle perhaps by buying the fruit from the garden of a retired gentleman. By day, they would earn their thirty shillings a week on a farm, in the evenings they would pick the fruit, leaving it outside their cottages for the local carrier to take to market first thing in the morning. Or they would grow sprouts on the allotment land in Carrants Field. If they had a bad year, they still had a wage to live on; good crops and good prices meant that they could save a little.

After some years, they might be able to afford to rent more smallholding land from the County Council or from a local landowner. They would then work three days a week for pay and three on the smallholding, eventually leaving paid employment to become 'little master men'.

The weather and prices were a constant anxiety. Their health and strength were also vital, so much was dependent on sheer muscle power, working the heavy clays with breast ploughs, and pushing handcarts loaded

A smallholder using a breast plough

with produce. Their wives put in countless hours, picking peas, bunching spring onions and gillyflowers, saving seed for the next year.

To see the old market gardener with his two-tine digger (two-pronged fork) cranked by the local blacksmith to suit his physique, every spit which he dug falling in the exact spot he intended, was a picture of skill.

I knew one of these gardeners who came to live in our village in 1897, Sam from Evesham. He wore cord trousers, yorks, with the inevitable peg tucked under one of them to clean his tools, and an Oxford shirt without collar summer and winter. In very hard weather he wore a muffler around his neck. He rented glebe land from the Church and planted a part of his six acres with strawberries and some with asparagus. He said that with these crops 'you got no seedsmen to pay every year'. So small was the margin of profit that at first he carried his asparagus in a hamper to within two miles of Evesham market or just over halfway and then went the rest of the journey by train.

The asparagus price was so low one year that some gardeners threw the bundles of asparagus into the Avon at Evesham Workman Bridge, while others fished them out again at Hampton Ferry. Sam's strawberries saved him, and when asked by the vicar of our parish how he lived, he replied, 'I've got my well and the ravens feed me like they did Elijah.'

The gardeners' squitch (couch grass) fires of March with the burnt sprout and cabbage stems produced quantities of red ashes. When this was mixed with pig manure and the contents of the earth closet and dug into the ground, it held the crops in a dry summer. But the gardeners were quick to realise the benefits of mineral fertilisers which they always called 'artificial'. 'Nitrogen is nitrogen whether it comes from Chile or out of a Hereford bull.'

Sam had his cider made at the cider mill at Hampton which, as well as cider, produced pomace which the gardeners dug in. The apple pips germinated and the young suckers were budded with the popular varieties of the day.

Farley Archer was a cousin of Grandfather Archer's and lived in a cottage adjoining the main Cheltenham road with his housekeeper, Polly Oliver. I knew him in the 1920s but he was hardly a typical smallholder of that time, in fact he was so primitive that he might have been Thomas Hardy's Grandfer Cantle in *The Return of the Native*. The cottage was not only occupied by Farley and Polly but by his hens and his cats. The hens roosted around his fireside, nested in his easy chairs, and Neddy, his donkey, was stabled in the little slated barn up the garden. Farley was quite a regular visitor to our house and as I picture him now in his working clothes (I never

A market gardener, an asparagus grower and their workers

saw him dressed up) I wonder whether he ever existed. His billycock hat
was tied on to his head with a piece of binder twine, probably to prevent it
falling off when he was working his land, about four acres in Carrants
Field. His other clothes were black gone green with age and his coat had
cloth-covered buttons. This was a typical funeral outfit of years back. When
he took off his coat he had underneath what was known as a ganzy or
cardigan, a mixture of black and white with buff-coloured bone buttons.
He was a stocky, upright man, like many of our family, about five feet eight
inches tall. Polly Oliver was deaf and dumb and short and stout; she wore a
brown hurden apron around her ample waist, carried a writing slate and
slate pencil wherever she went, and took snuff.

As Farley had only a donkey on his four acres he had a lot of hard work to
do, but we ploughed his land with our team of horses. Walt, our carter,
when he was having his bait sitting in the borough of Farley's hedge after
ploughing from just after seven o'clock in the morning, was surprised to see
Farley cross the main road from his cottage to his allotment carrying a large
jug. This was filled with cocoa with lumps of toast floating about on top.

'Yer thee bist, Walt, get that into tha. It will keep the cold out,' Farley said. As soon as Farley's back was turned Walt poured the mixture over the plough wheels. I don't think anyone could have relished any food or drink which came from that cottage. Enfield Cottage reeked of fermentation. Hogshead barrels sawn in half to make tubs stood in a little semicircle round the door out in the yard. These contained wines in various stages, parsnip, rhubarb, plum jerkum, all bubbling and fizzing. Fowls perched even on the rims of these tubs, the contents to be poured eventually into his barrels in the barn. Farley was often in a muddled state mixing his drinks. He kept a couple of hives of bees under the damson trees up the garden and after he had extracted the honey from the combs he boiled the honeycombs in water in his copper furnace, and next morning skimmed the beeswax off the top of the liquid and put the liquid in a little four-and-a-half gallon cask to become metheglin, a kind of mead.

Sometimes Polly Oliver came to our door with a message to my father written on her slate: 'Tom, 'ull you lend me a couple of men? We be gwain a-threshing tomorrow.' Dad usually obliged. Farley's threshing was a bit of a joke. He got the threshing tackle from a neighbouring village and Bertie Johnson had got steam up by seven o'clock in the morning waiting to start. 'Where be the men, Farley?' said Bertie. 'Don't know,' he replied. Bertie said, 'Hasn't axed anybody to come and help tha, Farley?' 'No, that I ant,' said Farley. 'They shouldn't need no axing. I'd a thought anybody uda come and helped me to thresh.'

His labels on his market produce caused many a laugh and he sent some runner beans into Evesham market one August labelled as four pots of Painted Ladies (the variety).

Farley's donkey died and he was soon at our house. He said he was all behind with his work already and he used this donkey with Polly leading it on his breast plough to clean his stubble, and harrow up the rubbish to burn. 'Tom,' he said to Dad. 'Ut thee send Walt down to skim a bit of ground ready for my runner byeans?' Walt went down with two horses, Prince and Bonnie, and the big two-wheeled skim and raised enough mould to plant the beans. Farley was busy digging a hole to bury old Neddy. 'He ant finished work for me yet,' Farley said, 'and I beunt a-gwain to put him in very dip.' Walt was thunderstruck at what he witnessed. Farley buried his donkey with his four legs sticking up in the air. Walt said, 'Why doesn't put him in dipper than that?' 'Ah,' said Farley, 'I be gwain to grow some runner byeans up his four legs this year.'

Farley could lay a hedge, dig a ditch, unstop a drain, but he was no builder. Two things he needed: one was a shed on his ground for shelter

A smallholder's family helping with the haymaking

and to keep his tools in; another was a privy up the garden. He built the shed first, and was priding himself on his workmanship when he needed the wheelbarrow to fetch his onions from the bottom of his ground. When he went to get the barrow it would not come through the door, and he had to knock down the side of his shed to get it out. He then built his privy, and again made the doorway so narrow that he had no room to turn round and had to reverse into it.

I suppose Farley and Polly had a fair living in their grubby way. They always kept a good pig and had a swill tub by the back door where all the cabbage-water leftovers and potato peelings went to add another unwhole-some smell to the surrounds of Enfield Cottage. They neither of them, Farley nor Polly, died of typhoid or food poisoning, and as far as I knew never had the doctor. Polly backed horses, and Farley studied the stars and both of them faded away with old age.

THE BOTTOM RUNG

In the 1920s the workers on the land were still looked upon as country yokels. Swede gnawers, a little bit lacking. This fallacy has been exposed by men like A.G. Street who knew that men who could plough, pitch hay and sheaves, layer hedges, shear sheep, milk cows, were skilled men, underrated and underpaid.

The farm labourers worked in gangs and received thirty shillings (£1.50) for a fifty-hour week. The only holidays with pay were Christmas Day and Good Friday. It did rile them that the council roadmen, who mowed the verges, swept the roads, earned a few shillings more, and also had Easter Monday as a paid holiday.

It was a real struggle to make ends meet, even with rents of three shillings (15p) a week, and those who had to pay higher rents hardly managed.

Poverty however was not so extreme in the country as it was in the towns. Each family had its pig, vegetables from the garden and an apple or plum tree. Agricultural labourers were careful with their twenty-nine shillings and threepence per week (ninepence went to pay for the National Insurance stamp). They grew potatoes, snared rabbits and with their wives gilly-picking in the spring, pea-picking in the summer, blackberrying for sale in the autumn and wooding in winter, they got by. There was also always the chance of overtime. Nevertheless, a few more shillings a week would have made all the difference on the bottom rung of the ladder.

Being right on the boundary between Worcestershire and Gloucestershire created another problem, as one county worked fifty-two hours for the same money as fifty hours worked in the next county.

There was, however, a will to work among the men of the land. In our village this was fostered, I'm sure, by the fact that the employers, 'the men as pays', took their own coats off and worked with the men.

Mr Carter (who died in 1936) had brought with him from Evesham a code, a pattern, which had to be followed. He carried neither tape measure nor pocket book, but knew instinctively whether a job was being done properly or not. These men of the old school worked by what was known as 'scowl of brow'; a term which simply meant experience, trial and error. And so I saw the men work with a will.

Stocky Hill

Stocky Hill was a member of a family which had lived in our village since the seventeenth century. He was a bachelor, a terrific worker able to cut an acre of wheat in a day with the two hooks, but he was more noted for his digging the heavy clay soil of the village. A chain or four hundred and eighty-four square yards with an Evesham Two Tine (two-prong) digger

Many smallholders and farm labourers had to rely on their health and strength to feed themselves and their families

The solemn, undertaker-like faces, the dark clothes, showed the world as they walked the half-mile village street carrying black bibles and hymn books that it was Sunday, the Lord's Day.

When the March winds blew clouds of dust up our village street a few years before the tar came to bind the road surface, crazes started.

eighty-four square yards with an Evesham Two Tine (two-prong) digger didn't come amiss to him. Job Barley, our under-cowman, used to describe him as a stomachful. He didn't mean Stocky was awkward, but that he could not give in or give up a job. There was nothing one would notice about his appearance in the late twenties. Wearing a black beaver hat, cord waistcoat and cord trousers, both of washed-out fawn, he was upright, broad-shouldered, a man who looked full of work yet. He was named Stocky for obvious reasons, Jasper, his brother, being head and shoulders taller.

He had a face which fairly bristled with whiskers, the beard kept fairly short. He smoked a pipe, usually a clay one, and the pleasant scent of Red Bell Shag on a frosty morning as he passed our house was in keeping with the countryside, and between the high-banked hedges of our lane it lingered in a blue-grey cloud.

He started courting at about sixty-five a servant girl of doubtful age from Cheltenham. Stocky used to take her back towards the big house in Cheltenham where she worked, walking with her to the Farmers Arms nearly at Bishops Cleeve. She pushed her bike and these Sunday nights Stocky walked about fifteen miles. In his own words he said, when he kissed her goodnight, 'That rattled just like a whip a-smacking!' On her days off Stocky and Ada did a part of their courting down the snaky, wandering lane known as Back Lane or Gipsies Lane.

Stocky was a man of few words. No wonder he had started courting very late in life and he had to learn. 'Why dosn't say summat?' Ada said one night. (The boys had followed them to catch every word.)

'What be I to say?' said Stocky.

'Why dosn't say as you loves me?'

'So I do,' said Stocky.

Ada followed up with, 'Don't the stars shine bright tonight?'

'Oi, they do,' replied Stocky.

This unusual courtship went on for some time and they thought of marriage. Stocky spoke to the vicar, who asked him the name of the lucky girl. 'Ada,' said Stocky.

The vicar said, 'I know that. What I want to know is her surname.'

'Lor bless the fella I couldn't tell tha. I allus calls her darling,' Stocky said in a rather superior tone. The vicar sorted things out and then trouble started. The Hill family thought it was a very unsatisfactory union and refused to have anything more to do with Stocky Hill. The old chap was furious, brought his bag of sixty golden sovereigns down to the village cross and, with the youths egging him on, said he had decided to broadcast his money there and then, and go and jump into the moat. 'Go on, Stocky, show um you means business,' they told him, but he put his money back in the poacher's pocket of his Derby tweed jacket, and walked up to the moat, the lads egging him on and saying, 'Show um you means business.'

There was no broadcasting of Stocky's sovereigns and he didn't jump in the moat, but the following Sunday morning Edward Hill and Ada Styles were asked in church for the first time. Stocky was persuaded to go, and when his name was read out he said in a loud stage whisper, 'Lors, that made I sweat,' mopping his brow with a clean red and white spotted handkerchief.

The wedding day arrived but Stocky was not an easy man to marry. When the vicar asked the question he answered 'Yes' instead of 'I will.'

'You must say "I will", Mr Hill,' the vicar insisted and Stocky came out with, 'All right then, if that's it, I will.'

Stocky could not sign his name in the register, only mark a cross. He and Ada did not come out of the church door, through the porch and down the churchyard. 'Oh no, my boy,' as Stocky told me later. 'I knowed they was a-waiting for us down in that lych-gate with their rice and their 'fetti, so me and the missis come out of the back vestry door and took the footpath across the field to the cottage.' The vicar asked Stocky about the honeymoon. Stocky said, 'Bless the fellow. We've already had that on Fuzz (Furze) Hill.'

Stocky was always in evidence at elections, firmly believing that things didn't go off as they should if there was no fighting, and he would try and start something of the sort for old times' sake, remembering the rowdy elections of his youth.

The Coalman

Jasper Hill was Stocky's younger brother and lived in the cottage next door. Tall and lean, he always looked the same, and seemed a fairly old man when I was a boy; yet he lived into the 1960s to the ripe old age of ninety. When he was seventy-odd he worked for me for two years but had been a coalman most of his life.

His wife Emma came as charwoman to our house. To say that Emma was careful would be an understatement. They lived on the bare minimum. Emma was a great believer in pastry lard, in fact, anything that was cheap. That and bread pudding was their staple diet. Jasper brought this for his mid-morning bait, washed down with cold tea without milk or sugar. Emma had no breakfast but had a cup of cocoa and plenty of bread and cheese at our house for lunch. She worked on the land in the afternoon, doing anything in season such as gilly-picking and onion and asparagus tying, and when the sprout stems from the previous year's picking had gone dry and hard in the stacks in the corner of the field she took some home every night in her blue and white cotton apron to burn under the boiler to do her washing. Soap she rarely bought, but took home in a little bag all the bits we had left as too small to use. Dr Overthrow told Jasper to drink plenty of barley water. Emma boiled the same barley twice. She said all the strength didn't come out first time.

One of the pleasures Jasper enjoyed in life was riding his bike. He had the same one for thirty years and got on a step on the hub of the back wheel. After a lot of scuffling and scooting he heaved himself into the saddle and was away.

Jasper's bike always shone and looked new; when he came in to tea Emma made him rub it over with an oil rag and hang it from the beams in his cottage before he was allowed to have his meal. If the day had been wet he had to give it a real good clean. Walt used to tell him, just to pull his leg, 'I should like to borrow thy bike tonight, Jasper. I got to go down to Beckford.'

'I specks not,' Jasper said. 'The missis won't let me lend him nobody.'

Football he was fond of and attended matches within cycling distance. He was at a match at Alderton one Saturday when a heavy storm came on rather suddenly. Jasper took off his top coat, covered his bike up and got wet through. Walt told him, 'Thee uds't never ketch cold. Thee bist too fulla pastry lard.'

At ordinary league matches in the Wynch there was no admission charge but at half time one of the committee went round with the box. Jasper, everyone noticed, kept his hands in his pockets almost up to his elbows as the wooden box was rattled in front of him. For hospital cup finals, semi-finals, and other big matches, threepence admission was charged at the horse pond stile. Jasper's garden ran right down to the football field in the Wynch and at the bottom of the garden by the low hedge was his one Victoria plum tree. To save threepence on these rare occasions Jasper climbed this tree and viewed the match from there. Some of the village lads knew all about this, and on the Saturday dinner-time before one cup final got some ticky-tack or banding grease and plastered Jasper's tree. How he got this off his trousers and what Emma said I don't know. Some of Jasper's comments at the home matches were a bit off-beat, and the referee was always wrong. You could hear old Jasper saying, 'How's he for offside, Ref? Dos't want to borrow my glasses?' He wore a pair of steel-rimmed ones well down his nose.

At cricket he liked to see a bit of action and if the runs didn't come quickly you would hear him. 'Mind thee doesn't break that bat.' 'They don't hit out like they used to years ago.'

He was always reminding me of years ago. 'That udn't a done in the Squire's time years ago.' In 1888, he said, 'it started freezing in November and we had sixteen wicks' frost in February!'

I said, 'That must have been a long February.'

'It was that. I never done no work all the winter except a wick or two's threshing.'

'How did you manage?'

Jasper said, 'We a'most lived on boiled swedes and taters and me and thee Uncle Jim at Christmas walked all round Bredon Hill with a melodeon and went carol-singing to the big houses. Some gen us vittle,' he said, 'others drink or money. About the end a March the weather took up, and me and thee Uncle George went wheat hoeing and we had a beautiful spring.' He was a handy man hoeing. He must have had a constitution like a horse. Walt said to him, 'If thee was to have a good meal a grub it ud kill tha.'

When he and Emma married it was on the rebound. Jasper had been courting Emma's sister Fanny and in his words, 'She chocked me up one Sunday night after Chapel in the little Sally Coppice next to the 'ood.'

When Fanny broke off with Jasper, they had already had the banns published, or 'bin asked in church'. The next couple to be asked in church was Jasper and Emma, just a few weeks after. When he got married he was working as carter on the Squire's farm and his work-mates teased him. 'They reckoned that I was obliged to but I knowed different. Just two years,' he said, 'afore the missis had the fust babby. Do you know what the gaffer (that was the Squire's bailiff) said? He said, "That un a bin a long while on the way, Jasper." It's all right. I knowed different.'

Going into his living room one Friday tea-time to ask him to come on the Monday and give a hand at threshing, I automatically took off my cap. 'Thee hadst no cause to take thee hat off, Fred lad. We beunt proud folks in yur.' It was rather gloomy inside the cottage. The windowsills were full of white geraniums which, as Job Barley, our cowman, said, 'had bin thur since the remembrance of mon', the floor was covered with newspaper to keep Jasper's hobnails off the scraps of lino. I noticed one window sealed up with paper and mentioned it to Jasper, 'Why should I spend my money on other folks' property?' came his reply quick, and to the point. The green-tasselled tablecloth was also partly covered with paper. 'I see you have a Sunday paper,' I said, rather surprised at the outlay.

'Oi,' he said, 'we do but the missis won't let me read him till Monday.' It was a popular one and Jasper's mind was not to be corrupted on Sunday, as he sat on the blue stone slab which formed a covering to the standpipe tap on the grass verge opposite his cottage.

Jasper's life would have been grim indeed but for the tips he collected with the coal money, which he took home to his wife. Emma would not allow him to smoke or drink, but he was given mugs of cider by the farmers when he delivered the coal, wine and Woodbines, known as 'freemans', by Pedlar. Sometimes he would treat himself, when he got a tip, to a packet of cigarettes. He kept these in the saddle bag of his bike. His wife found them and he was really on the carpet. The fellows at work used to put their butt ends in Jasper's saddle bag because Emma searched it every night when he came home.

One Christmas Jasper won a bottle of port wine in a draw. Mother said to Emma, 'What will you do with it? You don't drink.'

'We have a tablespoonful each before we go to bed,' said Emma, 'just for medicine.'

Among other things he grew in his garden was rhubarb which he was very proud of. He never gave much away. It was rumoured that he had had a good hiding as a boy for giving another boy something. One day as I was passing he was sitting in his usual place on the stone slab over the tap. He said 'Shouldst like a bit a rhubarb?'

'Yes, just enough to make a pie.' Jasper gave it me and I said, 'What good

Jasper Hill, the coalman, resting on the slab over the standpipe

rhubarb it is,' and he said, 'I'll let tha into a little secret. We allus empties the closet bucket on it.'

He was walking down to Church one Sunday with his stick with a horse's head handle which he had won at hoopla at Ashton Club. It was ten minutes to one. I said, 'Where you off so late, Jasper?'

He said, 'To Church. It wants about ten minutes to eleven.' Someone had told him to put the clocks back an hour instead of forward. He had no wireless. 'I didn't know we had to put um forrard this time,' he said, and he went home to get a late dinner. Another time a friend met him as he went to Church and told him it was very necessary for him to go, as he was a big sinner. 'No wus than anybody else,' he said, 'and besides it yunt allus them as goes to Church and Chapel as goes to heaven.'

I hope he's resting there. He was one of the most interesting people in our village. Apart from his coal-heaving, he scratched the top six inches of some of the farmland around Ashton for nearly eighty years.

The Poor

Ponto was a little man and he worked when he felt like it, doing jobs on the farms normally done by boys; leading horses at mangold and muck-cart, driving horses at plough, bird minding (bird scaring), running errands. Being simple-minded he was made a source of amusement by people who should have known better.

As a boy I was sometimes afraid when Ponto, then an old man, would be running after a group of lads who had been teasing him. When he worked for us he slept in a farm waggon in the cart shed, lived in the daytime in the little gear- or harness-room attached to our stable. Here he had his meals. We cooked his Sunday dinner and he cooked his usual midday meal, fried over a fire in the field. At tea-time he came to our window for a jug of tea, and he had several calling places in the village where they took pity on him and in this way he got by. He had a good appetite and when rationing was introduced during the 1914–18 war Ponto was in real trouble. He drew his week's rations from the village shop and got through the lot in about two days. When he went for more and was told he had had his allowance for that week, he kicked the door saying he 'allus had what he wanted when Mrs Hook kept the shop'. Dad then took over his ration card and doled his rationed food out day by day. He used to come to our back window in the summer-time and say to Mother, 'I be thirsty, mam, very thirsty.'

April Fool's Day was another opportunity to pull Ponto's leg. A farmer would put some stones in a sack and send Ponto with it to the next farm. This farmer would say a mistake had been made and send him in turn to the next. They would give him a drink of cider, and one wonders who was the bigger fool, the farmers or Ponto. Practical jokes of this kind are not funny but they had their place in the rough and tumble of village life as it was then. I shall always remember Ponto on the day of a funeral walking to Beckford and coming back along the road, drawing the four-wheeled truck which would be used to carry the coffin up the churchyard. Ponto never rode on this. He died in Evesham Workhouse and was buried in a pauper's grave.

It was when Dad was appointed Guardian of the Poor of our village that I first became deeply interested in that side of life, more especially workhouses. Seeing villagers go to these institutions gave me the feeling that people were being buried alive.

A man who sits, aged and drooling, on a grassy bank of a village street is in much more natural surroundings than in the carbolic prison house of an institution. Union workhouses catered for the poor of several parishes. Evesham had a Union Poor Law Institution, 'The Grubber' as it was called.

Two elderly villagers who relied on the parish for support

The Union Workhouse had a casual ward where tramps, travellers, stayed one night, had breakfast and were given a meal ticket, so that if they were walking to Tewkesbury or Cheltenham after their allotted task of work, they called at Beckford, exchanging the ticket for a slice of bread and cheese and a little tea. The permanent inmates, if married, met only in the gardens. The men worked in the gardens and fed the pigs with the swill from the kitchen. The women did housework. 'Whom God had joined together, let no man put asunder' didn't apply to the Poor Law. Old folk feared the workhouse. They used to say, 'They pulls the pillow from under yer 'ead there and finishes ya.'

As we were in Gloucestershire then and always had been in the Rural District of Pebworth, the Hundred of Tibalstone, Evesham was in a different county – Worcestershire.

Men and women of Ashton who became aged and infirm had been accepted at Evesham Union Workhouse without question. It must have been about 1928 when some genius of local government decided that Gloucestershire people from Ashton-under-Hill and Aston Somerville were being kept by Worcestershire rates.

Spider and Nathan, two Ashton men who had lived their lives on the land and slept in farmhouse bothies and out-buildings of the Star Inn, became unable to look after themselves. They went to Evesham Union Workhouse. Spider was happy in the gardens among the cabbages, Nathan fed the pigs.

After one meeting of the Board of Guardians, Dad and Lady Norah Fitzherbert found that four Gloucestershire men had been moved to Cheltenham. Lady Norah, being the representative for Aston Somerville, visited Cheltenham Workhouse. She found the men from the two parishes very unhappy. 'You see, ma'am,' Nathan told her, 'I allus looked upon the pigs at A'sum Workhouse as my charges.'

'Mr Archer, we must do something,' she told Dad. 'These men are heart-broken.'

Dad spoke to the Cheltenham Workhouse Master, who told him that he could release the men as casuals or vagrants and send them to Evesham. The Evesham Workhouse Master had to accept them. So one morning during the Easter Holiday, Dad drove the Sunbeam to the outskirts of Cheltenham and picked up four men walking the Evesham Road and brought them to our house. Mother had mugs of cocoa and bread, cheese and onions, and here I saw these men around our scrubbed kitchen table, as Dad put it, 'Just like schoolboys coming home on holiday.' He took them on to Evesham Casual Ward where they resumed their places among their friends.

The next Guardians' Meeting was stormy, as Lady Norah and Dad, who had flouted officialdom, had to explain the situation. The Guardians allowed the men to stay and three years later in 1931 Ashton was transferred to Worcestershire, so the problem never arose again. You have no idea how proud I was of Dad on the day Spider and Nathan came back, but had he studied the parish records, as I have done since, his case for their admission to Evesham Union would have been undisputed.

It is clear from these records that in 1860 eight cottages were sold in Ashton parish to raise money for the Evesham Union, and that our village set up a fund to pay for its share of the expense of building it.

As Guardian, Dad, who had lived in our village all his life, knew the people pretty well. One February day, I went with him to see Bill Allen, aged and crippled with rheumatism. Bill, or Blenheim as he was called, had worked his life away on the land until he was unable to crop the hedges, dig the ditches of the farms. His pension of ten shillings per week was not sufficient to keep body and soul together. He, more than anyone, was entitled to some relief.

'Come with me, Bill,' Dad said, 'and see the Relieving Officer.'

After some persuasion he got in the car.

'I beunt a gwain on the Parish mind, Master Archer,' he told Dad. 'I don't fancy being beholden to nobody.'

Dad said, 'I understand, Bill, but it's different now. The Relieving Officer will be sympathetic to your case.'

If a man and his wife lived together they could just manage on one pound per week, but with Bill being a bachelor it was different.

Bill put on his dark overcoat, the one, I fancy, he had worn to carry the coffin at funerals when one of his generation passed on. We went to Evesham and of course he was given a few shillings to tide him over. When the weather took up, Bill was back in the fields hoeing the peas and sprouts of the village. When he died the next year, he had saved enough in a stocking to pay for his funeral. Bill didn't want to be beholden to the parish.

It's a heartening thought how much pride and independence such men had, and how much they appreciated dying in their own beds under the thatch after a lifetime of sunshine and storm.

I well remember the smell of cow manure on Harry Flute's boots as he sat in our kitchen while Dad filled in his pension form, Harry's bristly chin, his cidery breath, his chuckle when he said, 'I be no scollard, Master.'

Never having known hunger myself, I mixed and talked with men who had. 'Give us this day our daily bread' meant something to them. Bread to them was sacred. To waste a crust was a crime. It seems a long while ago.

4

The Outside World
Comes to Ashton

THE OUTRIGHTS

When I was a boy, our old farm workers had an unusual name for people who came round the village from the town shops, stores and warehouses taking orders for goods; they called them the 'Outrights'. Perhaps this was a variation on the word 'Outrider', but anyway they were travellers or 'representatives' as we would call them today.

Most of the Outrights cycled, some came by horse and trap, others by train, and one or two had cars. Hubert from Tewkesbury was in the grocery trade; he cycled over every other Friday to get the order to be delivered by horse and van the next Tuesday. He travelled round most of the villages within eight or nine miles of Tewkesbury. He was a tall, upright man, smartly dressed in Norfolk jacket, breeches and stockings with boots well 'Cherry Blossomed'; military in bearing with a fierce-looking waxed moustache.

Hubert Outright, or Harding, had a good round in our village. He had become a household word; people seldom thought of giving him up, and he had served my grandfather and the Bradfields long before the 1914 war. One of his best customers was Charlie Bradfield who had a large family; Hubert arrived there about tea-time and Charlie started off:

'Now, Master Hubert, I a got a bone to pick along a you.'

'Have you, Charlie, now what's the trouble?'

'I'll be dalled if you didn't send us some cheese last fortnit – what did the Mussus order – five pounds, wasn't it? – and you sent us eight.'

'Sorry about that, Charlie.' Hubert looked really worried. 'It's the girls in the shop. It won't happen again and there's a pint of cider paid for you at the Plough.'

A grocer's shop in Beckford, which would have sent 'Outrights' to the villages to take orders for goods

It happened again but the pint was always up at the Plough for Charlie. Tom Wheatcroft described Hubert as 'a generous mon; he treated all as was in the Plough every other Friday night'.

It was about eight o'clock when he arrived at our house. He knocked loudly on our front knocker (he was deaf) and this started our two dogs barking. Dad took the candle to the door to let him into the hall, then into the oil-lit living room. It there was rain or a cold wind blowing, Dad bawled into his ear, 'What a terrible night.'

'Yes, yes, yes,' Hubert answered, 'not like I suffered on the Somme though.'

As he sat by our fireside with just enough cider in him to make him talkative, he related some of his experiences. I shoved my homework book on one side as Hubert said, 'I started soldiering in the Royal Horse Artillery before I went in the trenches.' He described in detail the shells, the leather covered traces of the horses, the hubs on the gun carriage wheels and Hubert in puttees, spurs and tunic; and we learned how the noise of the guns made him deaf.

'Many rats about in the corn ricks, Mr Archer?' he asked Dad.

'We don't grow any corn now, Hubert,' Dad again cupped his hand and hollered into Hubert's earhole.

'Ha, I suppose it's the foreign stuff being so cheap, but you boys' (he turned to me and my brother) 'have never seen rats.'

'I've seen rats,' said Hubert (the cider was working), 'bigger than a cat in the trenches on the Somme.' We had rats in the outhouse where the fowl corn was kept and later on in the evening I had to go up there with a candle to fetch the fire-lighting wood for morning. If ever I see one tonight, I shall have a blue fit, I thought.

'Now, Mrs Archer, your order,' Hubert said, undoing a piece of black garter elastic from around his little blue book. 'Flour, self-raising, currants, sugar . . . ' he went through the lot. One week he said, 'Pepper,' and cupped his ear.

'No, not this week,' Mother said.

'Pepper's going up,' said Hubert. 'Just in confidence it's going to be dear. Some of the big businesses are cornering it, get plenty of pepper in now you have the chance.' Mother ordered a small quantity but I imagined her ordering enough to fill a Huntley and Palmers biscuit tin.

Hubert prided himself on their tea, 'Specially blended for the waters of the district, your water's got a lot of lime in it, you know,' he said. 'I take so much Darjeeling, so much Ceylon and it's a blend second to none.'

For three fortnights Mother had not ordered tea and Hubert became suspicious. Mother had to admit that Dad, who was a martyr to indigestion, had fancied a brand reputed to prevent it. Hubert was not mollified.

Another week Mother ordered sauce and forgot to state the size of the bottle. Hubert send a cafe size! It stood on our breakfast table pointing to the ceiling like one of Hubert's guns. But Hubert was a good man to both his employers and his customers. I fancy if a family fell on hard times he would help to foot the bill, keeping them afloat until the tide turned. I don't expect he ever realised that he did a little to break the monotony of some people's winter evenings.

Bastin's were known in Evesham as shoe and boot makers. The trade in made-to-measure shoes and boots was almost dead when I was a boy, but Bastin's still did some for old customers. Bastin's had their Outright who must have been one of the last of the packmen. He called at our house with his pack of boots for the farmworkers, hob nailed, tea-drinkers (light boots for Sunday), and brands known as Little Dukes and Little Gents for us boys. I felt no end of a fellow when I wore my first pair of Little Gents, laced, with holes half way, then hooks for the top two or three rows. He also carried cotton and leather laces, shoe polish, and dubbin which was a very necessary part of a farm worker's gear. I have seen our cowman with a pair of Bastin's Plough and Harrow boots plastered in dubbin, stand in the horse trough with the water up to near the top of the lace holes. Leather was waterproof, it had to be, there were no rubber wellington boots. Farm workers anticipating winter's rough weather invested their harvest money in leather boots. Bastin's Outright also took boots in for repair, but he was particular, the boots had to be their own brand.

One Outright I well remember, a Mr Marks, who sold fertiliser. He came round in a two-seater car and dicky, was immaculately dressed in a light grey suit and had a carnation in his button hole. Dad bought 'artificial', as we called it, by the truck load – smelly Peruvian guano, meat and bone, fish manure, and Mr Marks sold the lot. He, like Hubert, was deaf but he had a hearing aid; one wit said that you shouted in one ear for sulphate of ammonia and in the other for superphosphate. If Dad ordered three tons of artificial, Mr Marks with his book out would say, 'Make it five tons, it comes cheaper,' and he would write down five. Sometimes Dad would say, 'All right then, but don't send it until I send you a postcard, the artificial house is almost full.'

What a senseless way they had of packing these fertilisers in those days – always in two-hundredweight bags which had to be manhandled out of the railway vans, and oh, the smell of some of it! It was definitely not artificial to me. The meat and bone was coarse ground, with bits of cow horn clearly visible in the bags; the fish was beyond description. Mr Marks sold nothing but the best, and his breezy, cheerful personality inspired the growers in our Vale. When prices in the market were good, the growers really ploughed their profits back into the ground. Mr Marks was not a high-pressure salesman, but a good adviser of the best manure to use; he had to meet his customers again on market day.

THE PEA-PICKERS

During the 1920s Mr Carter and Dad grew a large acreage of peas. From the first week in February, if the ground was in the right condition, a succession of planting took place during the spring and summer, from the round-seeded Early Bird until the final plantings of Senator and Lincoln, which were planted on the flat top of Bredon. The late peas were planted there because the breeze which usually blows on the hill doesn't encourage mildew like the damper Vale with its autumn fogs.

Pea-pickers on Tom Archer's land

The first pickings have been on 31 May and the last on Armistice Day. The pea-pickers were a mixed lot. They arrived in May, that is, the travelling type. Staff and Aggie were usually first, and dossed down in the first pigsty next to the trap house. Some, like these two, had just enough money to tide them over until picking started. The casuals, or 'roadsters' we called them, were later reinforced with the Cheltenham Lower Dockham crowd, who left their houses and lived in 'bivvies' or tents of sacking under the hedges when all the buildings were full.

We never knew their real names, and called them after their place of birth: Staff (Staffordshire), Brummie (Birmingham), Cock (London), Manchester, Scottie, Devon. The others had to have some means of being identified, and were called Joe, the Doings, Darkie (a Suffolk navvy who lived in the Cross Barn with Scottie, who had been first engineer on an ocean liner), Mick and Jim. Then there was a little man with rough whiskers and a rougher dog; and Annie Shaw from Lancashire. Trotting Johnny trotted everywhere compared with Hopping Annie, a woman with a wooden leg and a filthy tongue. Little George lived at Great Hill Barn and came down on Saturday for his pay and shopping.

In those days all our cattle were at grass for the summer and the pickers took over the farm outbuildings. They were a motley crowd with barefooted children – I remember one whose father was a widower left with a four-year-old boy, a sweet little chap. Our old Light Sussex cockerel used to chase him across the yard to our back door, where Mother used to dry his tears and give him a sweet. If his father was near and the little fellow didn't say 'Thank you' straight away, he'd say, 'Mind yer manners, my boy, in front of Godly folk and gentry.'

The tragedy of all this to me was that lots of these roadsters had fought through the First World War and came to this precarious life. It was different with the Lower High Street lot from Cheltenham; they had homes of sorts to return to in the autumn. Tom Wheatcroft and I were horse-hoeing sprouts near the main road one day just as the hordes of broken men and women were on their way from Evesham to Cheltenham or Tewkesbury Workhouse (or the 'Grubber' as he called it). I complained about some small thing and Tom said, 'Oi, the hardest work thur is, my boy, is to carry an empty belly along that turnpike road.'

The pickers were paid a shilling for forty pounds of peas, picked either into a pot bag or a pot hamper. Uncle George weighed the peas from a tripod, made from larch poles by Oliver, with a chain to suspend the spring balances. For every pot which weighed forty pounds the picker was given a cheque with 'HC' stamped on it, the initials of Harry Carter, Dad's partner. This worked very well, because it meant that Uncle George had no money on him, and the pickers could change their cheques when they needed the money by coming to our bay window overlooking the courtyard. We always knew whom to expect after tea. Staff and Aggie, Sacko and Manchester were regulars, but Scottie and Darkie would not lower themselves to change their cheques every night; they came with the regular men for their wages on Friday nights.

We were always pleased to see Scottie arrive about Whitsun with his few belongings in his bag. He kept himself spotlessly clean, and after a few weeks' work bought himself a new hard-cloth jacket and a pair of cord trousers. He blacked his boots and waxed his moustache on Sundays and walking up our village street, with little puffs of smoke coming from his pipeful of twist, he was the aristocrat of the pea-pickers. On summer nights, as he and Darkie cooked their meals under the Warner's King apple tree at the back of the Cross Barn, he took 'the chair' at a pea-pickers' parliament, and he was a treat to listen to. I have heard of Keir Hardie; I imagine he may have been of the same kidney. Scottie detested strong drink but was a great gambler. Over his bed, which was partitioned off from the others in the barn by hurdles, he had written in copperplate writing, 'He who steals my purse steals trash.'

The Cheltenham crowd came for a good time, fresh air, a paid holiday, and an evening singsong at the pub. As our stock of shillings disappeared when cheques were changed, Dad sent me to John Collins at the pub with five pounds to ask him to give me a hundred shillings. A lot of these shillings had been spent by our pea-pickers and as old Charlie Bradfield said, 'Money is made round and it goes round.' In the cool bar on a summer evening as John counted out the hundred shillings, I read in letters of gold over the fireplace these words: 'As a bird is known by its note so is a man known by his conversation. Swearing strictly prohibited.' It struck me that a landlord of days before the pea-pickers came in their hundreds had put that up for local benefit. I mixed and mingled with people of all sorts. There were usually a hundred picking.

At the pub the singing was something out of this world as Caruso tried to outdo Paul Robeson and Gracie Fields competed with Melba. I listened from my bedroom window as *The Shade of the Old Apple Tree* changed to a piece by Gilbert and Sullivan. At closing time all were friendly and in our backyard I heard so often, 'Goodnight, Titch. God bless. We are pals, mind.' Then Joe, the Doings, would call him back and, with a hand on the shoulder, say, 'No offence to what I said. God bless, Titch.' This was repeated by the pickers as they returned to their separate stalls, a few at a time.

We seldom had any trouble on or off the field but I vividly remember one July night at about eleven-thirty a squeal like murder coming from the lidded place at the end of the barn. Dad lit his candle and as Mother said, 'Do be careful, Tom,' he put an overcoat on top of his night-shirt, went downstairs in his slippers and found Joe the Doings, fast asleep in Annie Shaw's manger.

When Annie, a reputed spinster, arrived home from the pub to find him there, she squealed and squealed. A few words from Dad and all was quiet again as I leant out of my back bedroom window. Dad was quite unafraid of the pickers and they treated him with respect.

As the summer fled by and only the Lincolns on Bredon remained to be picked, the roadsters packed their bags, loaded their prams and went for another year. Scottie and Darkie were usually the last to leave and we were sorry to see them go. Scottie brought a little of the outside world into our village.

5

Magic and Mystery

Bredon Hill has been a place of magic and mystery since the time of the Druids. Ashton folk were reared on a mixture of the superstitions and folk wisdom of old Gloucestershire. The older workers still drew the sign of the cross with a shuppick on a pile of seed corn to keep the devil away. They would sooner go cold than burn elderberry wood, which they thought would bring the devil down the chimney. They would not kill a pig nor sow seed when the moon was on the wane, nor let a woman during her monthly handle the bacon while it was curing.

The King and Queen stones which stood on the escarpment of Bredon Hill were thought to have healing powers if you passed between them. A hot cross bun, baked the year before, was taken as a remedy for some ailments.

When a deal was struck at Gloucestershire markets by the striking of the palm of the hand, the bargain was clinched with luck money. If the dealer did not receive luck money when he bought from the farmer, the farmer was supposed to have bad luck with his stock at home.

There were tales of hauntings around Bredon Hill and in the oldest houses in the village. The marsh lights down by Carrants Brook were eerie enough to unsettle a grown man and were spoken of as Bobbity Lantern's Will o' the Wisps.

I have always been intrigued by the mysterious and by mysteries. There is something in delving into things which can't be understood that gives a certain satisfaction.

There were two men in the village, Joe Baker and the doctor, who both seemed to me to be involved in magic and mystery in their different ways.

THE WATER DIVINER

Water divining is a gift, you either have it or you haven't. Joe Baker was a mystic. He was a water diviner extraordinary. 'Some folks thinks I have got

The King and Queen stones on Bredon Hill

a tile loose,' he told me one day. 'Just because I have learnt a few things without ever rubbing my back against a college wall.'

A nearby small town was short of water and Joe Baker said there was any amount up on Spring Hill, about three-quarters of the way up Bredon. One Saturday afternoon in midwinter Joe, accompanied by Dad, Mr Carter and me, started to climb the hill with one object in view, to find enough water to supply the town of Pershore. We all knew the springs which flowed constantly out of the mounds covered with rough wiry grass on the northern slopes of Spring Hill, but Joe said there was also an underground stream on the south side. When I said he was a water diviner extraordinary, what I meant was that he did not use a forked stick and hold the two-forked end to find water. He had copper wires around his arm and from these he suspended a pendulum made from the golden top of an umbrella filled with mercury. When he was standing over a subterranean stream the golden knob rotated in a certain way.

We walked through Paris gardens, a hamlet on the lower slopes, past the barn and up on to the Leasows, where Mr Carter bowled over a rabbit with his twelve bore. He paunched and hocked the rabbit and gave it me to carry.

We reached Spring Hill at about three o'clock and Joe Baker got ready his dangler, as he called it. From the Leasow gateway he followed the horse road for about a hundred and fifty yards and nothing happened with his strange device. He then made a sharp left-hand turn towards Grafton Firs and soon the golden knob began to rotate, slowly at first, then gathering momentum until Joe stopped almost on his knees on a knoll near a few hawthorn trees, stunted by the poorness of the ground. As Joe stood there trembling he explained that it was taking energy from his body and he had to restrict his divining to allow him to get back this energy.

He told Mr Carter and Dad that he would not advise sinking a well there and that there were better places ahead. In single file with me bringing up the rear, we followed this imaginary water course for about two hundred yards, Joe Baker sometimes walking in circles and sometimes in almost a straight line. When the water was near the surface Joe was brought to his knees and the golden ball rotated like a seat in one of the chairplanes that I had seen at Evesham Mop.

In a hollow shaped like a basin, at the foot of a steep bank alive with rabbits, Joe stopped a long time. 'Thousands of gallons of clear spring water,' he said, 'are pouring under my feet, quite shallow too. Now if you want to dig to find plenty to supply Pershore, there is abundant water here, and with the two springs on the northern slope a reservoir could be made.' We were about eight hundred feet above sea level so there would have been no difficulty about fall, the town being on the River Avon. Both Dad and Mr Carter were now almost as sure as Joe that by just digging down a few feet the water would gush out from this stream yet unseen. I stood there, a raw youth with a rabbit, expecting at any time to see rabbits produced from hats. I said nothing, just listened. 'What about it, Tom?' Mr Carter said to Dad. 'Shall we send old Oliver and Taffy up Monday morning and start to sink a shaft?'

'All right, Harry,' Dad said to Mr Carter, 'but they will want some timber before they get too deep.'

Mr Carter said, 'Right. We'll send Walt with a much-cart and two horses to take their tackle up.' Up until now Joe Baker had been successful in finding water in several villages round the Vale with his dangler.

Monday morning came, and as it was the school holiday I went with Walt and the horses and cart, and took Oliver's and Taffy's tools and timber up to the basin-shaped hollow on Spring Hill. Instead of digging a round well-shaped hole they dug a square shaft and struck the Cotswold limestone only inches under the turf. With pick axes and shovels, spades and grafts, they pressed on. First there was a layer of stone, then shale and gravel as hard-packed as rock. When they came to a very large stone they dug round it, loosened it with their crowbars and then hauled it up on a rope.

At the end of January, when I was back at school, Taffy, whose pale blue eyes fairly sparkled when he looked up out of the deepening shaft, came to our bow window overlooking the courtyard. It was about seven o'clock in the evening and I was doing my homework. There was a knock at the back door and I went to open the window with a candle in my hand. Taffy's eyes sparkled in the light of the candle but I had seen nothing yet. 'I say, mun, can I see your father quickly? We have struck gold on Spring Hill.' I ran back into the kitchen where Dad was reading *The Echo* and told him. Out of his jacket Taffy brought out several nuggets about the size of cricket balls which sparkled in the candlelight. Dad said, 'It looks like some sort of gold to me. Fred, take a piece to school in the morning and ask the chemistry master.'

That night, as we sat around our old oven grate in the kitchen and handled these nuggets, I thought of what I had read of the Klondike and the Gold Rush and whether anything of the sort would or could happen here. That night I could hardly sleep with excitement.

On the eight-fifty train I met the usual friends and told them what I had in my satchel. 'Let's just have a look at it before you show it to Dapper,' they said. I unbuckled my satchel and undid the brown paper parcel and the nugget was handed around the carriage.

We didn't have chemistry that day so I asked Dapper at break, 'Please, sir, could you tell me what this is?'

One look and he said, 'Fools' gold – copper pyrites. Where did you find it, Archer?' I told him it was about fifteen feet down a shaft on Bredon. I kept it for a bit along with other junk in my drawer hoping he was wrong.

At twenty feet down the shaft there was still no sign of water and Dad got a bit tired of Taffy and Oliver digging up there when they could have been hedge-cutting and fencing, their usual winter jobs, and the dig was called off. Joe Baker, naturally disappointed, used to take his dangler down the shaft and round and round it went, faster than ever. We shall never know whether if they had dug perhaps only another six feet into the now fairly solid rock, the much sought-after water would have oozed out to make Taffy and Oliver beat a hasty retreat.

Joe Baker, besides being able to divine water, claimed also to be able to find coal, salt and human skeletons. He used to practise on the last up in the churchyard. He had other fandangos, as Job Barley called them, for divining, which rang little bells. I shall never forget how he demonstrated at a local flower show and said there was oil underneath an orchard.

On one of our Sunday School outings to Barry, Joe sat in the back seat with some of his equipment. We were travelling in our village twenty-seater bus. As the bus took us past Gloucester, Chepstow and beyond, Joe could be heard every so often, 'My word, there's some water here.' Then, 'Now we are over coal' or 'oil' or whatever the bell rang for. We enjoyed this part of the outing quite as much as the fun-fair and candy-floss of Barry.

Joe was a man of many parts. We had all seen Joe's deft hands as a bone setter putting right dislocated knees and shoulders on the football pitch.

He could be very serious when he taught us at Sunday School. He had been a shepherd as a young man and told us of the Good Shepherd. 'I often wonder,' he would say, 'what will become of you boys when you grow into men. Now don't get swelled-headed when you are fourteen and think you are men and too old to come here,' he'd say. He used to tell us of the dire poverty of his boyhood. His father was a drunkard and treated his wife and children very badly. He recalled how he drove oxen to plough on Bredon at ten years of age. He had no jacket, just a sack over his shoulders, and with hands raw with chilblains he washed in the morning at the roadside tap in icy water. 'Fred lad,' he told me, 'my father used to play the fiddle round the pubs for drink but he hung the fiddle up at our door and beat my poor mother.' He said, 'Never hang your fiddle up at the door,' which I thought was good advice. 'I could take you to a cottage,' he said, 'where one wall is marked with bacon fat where my father threw the frying pan at Mother in a drunken bout.'

Joe learned to read and write from his wife after he married. He learned to read the Bible and knew it very well. He talked a lot about Job, how he scraped the sores off his body with a ploughshare. To an extent, I suppose, Joe Baker as a boy had suffered like Job.

Joe Baker played the big bass viol at Chapel and had a mellow bass singing voice. He could remember the orchestra playing the music from the Church gallery. At concerts and social evenings Joe would give an exhibition with the bones to piano accompaniment. He also played the tin whistle and recited:

'I comes up from the country but I beunt so very green.
I knows that two and two be four and twice four beunt eighteen.
I reads a lot of things in books. I learned a bit at school.
Folks tries to do me but I does they. Because I looks a fool.'

At the evening Chapel meeting he took the place of a preacher who failed to turn up. 'Stop-gap Baker, that's me. I'm here to stand in the breach.'

He was unequalled as a grafter of fruit trees. Somewhere between ninety and a hundred per cent of them grew. He did it the only way common in his time, plastering the joint with puddled blue clay after he had tied his grafts in with raffia. As a pruner of trees he was an authority and some nicely balanced trees today are the result of his training.

When he was gardener up at the Close he became well known for his roses. I also remember him turfing lawns. He had a turfing iron which shone like silver. Then he beat the turf into shape with a home-made tool like a flat square beetle.

What couldn't Joe Baker do? The only thing I didn't see him do was thatch a rick. He could build one. I remember Joe Baker, with a straw boater covered with a net, his face covered, his hands gloved, a straw skep in his hand, going out on a June evening to take a swarm of bees. He kept many hives of bees and when they swarmed in all sorts of odd places, Joe Baker would take them.

One summer's evening, Mr Carter, some of the men and young Bert Bradfield were coming down Bredon after a hard day's work among the sainfoin, pitching and loading the waggon and ricking it by the Great Hill Barn. On the Barn Hill, which had not been cut for hay, Bert, who had eyes like a hawk, spotted something shaped like a rugby football on top of a large boar thistle. 'Master Carter,' he said, 'yer's a swarm of bees.'

'My boy,' said Mr Carter, 'tell Joe Baker when you get home and bring him up and help him to take them. I expect he will give you a shilling.' Bert came up late that evening with Joe and they took the swarm.

'Master Carter said you'd give me a shilling, Master Baker, but I beunt a-going to axe you for it.'

Joe Baker said, 'Oh ah.' He didn't give him the shilling but he paid his fare for a day trip to Weston-super-Mare the following week.

Joe was a man of principle. As he told us at Sunday School, if a man asks you to go a mile, go two. Whether he was laying a hedge, building a rick, budding a rose or grafting, you could depend the job was done right. There was no need to find any tools for him. He had a tool for every job he did. There is still a Pitmaston Duchess pear tree that Joe grafted on a hawthorn tree many, many years ago. He died getting on for twenty years more than the allotted span and worked until his end, which was peace.

THE VILLAGE DOCTOR

Edward Overthrow was the village doctor at Ashton-under-Hill for about forty years until his death in 1928. I knew him well when I was a boy.

Besides being the owner of Rockland House, formerly his wife's family home, he had several more properties in the village. Pear Tree Cottage, named after the giant pear tree in the garden overlooking the road, was his surgery.

I watched the doctor working in his surgery under a window which was close to the roadside footpath. He appeared mystical to me as he mixed his medicines over a sink with a bucket of water beside him. His closely clipped King Edward VII beard under a grey moustache stained with nicotine fascinated me and fired my imagination; the smoking cap smacked of the East. Was he a miracle man? Did his medicines grow from the herbs of the hill? He counted aloud as he mixed one spot of coloured liquid out of one bottle with a number of spots of some other potion. I could hear him counting. The now shaking hand of a man of eighty allowed one spot too many to fall into the enamel bowl. 'Damn and blast,' he called out as he threw the whole mixture down the sink and started again to spot the potions into the measured spring water in the bowl.

This time he poured the mixture into a funnel which he fixed into the neck of the medicine bottle, filled the bottle and stuck on a label with

Edward Overthrow, the village doctor, in his trap pulled by Violet. The man on the left is Joe Baker, the water diviner

instructions on it. He then covered the bottle with white paper, melted some sealing-wax to seal the edges, and someone's prescription was ready for collection. At six o'clock the villagers collected their cough mixtures, their jalap, and indigestion mixtures reeking of peppermint. 'Tell your father to give the bottle a thundering good shaking before he takes his medicine, boy,' I remember him saying.

There was something about the doctor's medicine which relieved symptoms even if it didn't cure the patient. Men on the land would say, 'I've been pretty middling lately. I'll have to get another bottle of the doctor's jalap.' Old villagers who were patients of Dr Overthrow were adamant that his prescriptions and patient care cured them of many serious illnesses. 'A clever man,' some said. 'A long headed man,' said others. I don't think he was a genius, but a good practitioner in his time. His time was past when I knew him. He had not kept up with the more modern approach to medicine.

At the doctor's surgery things were primitive. He had to carry the water to mix his medicines from a roadside standpipe – I've seen him standing there with a bucket under the tap waiting for it to fill.

The surgery itself had little of the modern fitments of a man of medicine. A bare deal table, a brown crock sink, bare whitewashed walls with shelves stocked with medicines. Large blue bottles marked 'Poison', measuring glasses, funnels, a pestle and mortar, in fact everything an early twentieth-century doctor stocked. Empty medicine bottles, white paper, sealing-wax, a steel-nibbed pen and an ink pot. Here he worked in velvet jacket and smoking cap – a wizard.

Sam, a farmer and innkeeper, passed by the surgery one day. He was on the School Board with the doctor. 'Sam,' the doctor called from his window. Sam walked into the surgery and sat down on a wooden chair beside the doctor, thinking that some business of the school was to be discussed. 'Have a drop of whisky,' the doctor offered.

'Ah, I will have one with you,' Sam replied. From the very top shelf Edward reached down a blue bottle marked 'Poison'. 'I'm not having any out of there,' Sam said in a state of panic.

'Why, I have to mark my whisky "Poison" or else other members of the family will drink it and leave none for me,' was the reply.

He had one, I think, quite unique trait. He was a good visitor because he came at night. When he sat at the bedside of some old villager and talked, that did tend towards healing. It's true he talked even longer through the night if the man's wife was liberal with her home-made wine. His theory was, 'See your patients at night, see them at their worst.'

I've seen the doctor often at night in the village. To be more precise, I've seen a man in black hurrying to a patient, holding in his hand a jam jar with a short candle glowing like a glow-worm. In his other hand he held his Gladstone bag with all the mysteries of his profession. He muttered to himself as he walked. His soft leather boots made little noise; they squeaked their way over the rough limestone lane. His day, or should I say his night, had only just begun. I would stand on the grass verge as he passed. He was the village oracle, magic. In the dim light of his candle I'd sometimes see Sailor following his master. It was always said in the village that even in a howling gale his candle never went out. That bothered me as a boy and made me wonder whether this man was a witchdoctor.

The consulting room at Rockland House was to the right of the great oak door. It was an elegant room, furnished with his grandfather's suite, the polished mahogany table standing in the centre under an oil-burning chandelier. The fireplace was graced with *petit point* screens decorated with swans, kingfishers and woodpeckers, and in the corner his leather sofa awaited patients. The tools of the trade were kept on shelves in a little anteroom at the back: forceps, scissors, bandages, tooth drawing instruments, all the first aid equipment of the day. Only medicines were kept in the surgery.

While hedge-cutting one day, Walt the carter ran a long thorn into the middle of his hand. The hand turned septic, as often happened with blackthorn. After a restless night Walt plucked up courage to see his doctor. 'It needs lancing, hold your hand out,' the doctor ordered and took a pair of scissors off the shelf in the anteroom, scissors which were anything but sharp. One or two attempts to cut the proud flesh failed until at last the great blister broke, the poison falling onto the polished mahogany table. 'Damn and blast,' the doctor shouted, and Walt, with the pain relieved, felt it to be his fault.

Dr Overthrow's way of dress was a much a mark of his profession as the corduroys of the men of the fields. When out with the gun and Sailor, his spaniel dog, Doctor Edward looked like the farmers of the village, dressed in tweeds and a soft hat, but his dress while on his rounds was that of a Victorian city gentleman. He wore a box hat, a cross between a top hat and a bowler. These were in vogue at the turn of the century. Above his closely cropped beard and moustache his cheeks were rosy. He wore a long black jacket with four cloth-covered buttons, a white shirt with a starched 'Come to Jesus' collar, and a bright red cravat with a golden tie-pin. His black waistcoat was chained from buttonhole to pocket by a golden Albert, a chain hung with sovereigns. The doctor's pinstriped black and white

Club day in Ashton. Joe Baker is second from the left in the fourth row back

trousers clipped him below the knee, and were shaped narrow to the ankle. His shoes were what some folk call high lows, they were neither boots nor shoes. They were black leather with elastic at the side. Around his ankles in winter-time he wore spats of a felt material. On his rounds in the village he carried a Gladstone bag and he walked with a silver-mounted walking-stick. The man was impressive, he scared me, but how the old folk loved him. He commanded respect. He was a handsome man even in old age. No wonder he had such success as a ladies' man in his youth. His smart appearance seemed to give confidence to his patients.

Mrs Lippet who did his washing and also did ours used to tell a tale about the doctor's shirts. She said that he cut the tail off his shirts for bandages. 'Nair a bit of tail on any of his shirts, Master,' she told Dad. There would be emergencies, but a shirt tail for bandages?

Thomas Packer of Cheltenham was a great friend of Dr Overthrow and it was he who started the Sick and Dividend Society in 1876. Dr Overthrow was the official doctor who vetted the members for what was known as 'The Club.' It was bad luck if a member fell ill during the first months of the year, for there was little in the kitty to pay out benefit. Every Christmas the Club members met at the Star Inn and shared what was left of the year's income.

The Club Feast, held on Trinity Monday, began with a service in St Barbara's church. The members then marched with their brass-mounted staves up the village street to Corse Lawn band. Every farmer, almost every householder, placed jugs of beer or cider on their garden walls for the members to refresh themselves. The feast was held in a marquee in the Plough and Harrow yard, and here Edward Overthrow took the chair, accompanied by the vicar and John Bostock, and toasts were proposed.

The Club provided a safety net for the folk stricken with ill-health. When a few young men in their teens asked to join, Dr Overthrow arranged a vetting in his consulting room. The figure of Edward in black cloth-buttoned jacket and pinstriped trousers standing in this room with its thick, flowery wallpaper, old suite and leather couch, commanded respect from the villagers. The youths stood apprehensive in the hall. The curtains of the consulting room remained undrawn, and a knot of impish, inquisitive youths peered through the window as Edward vetted the potential Club members. They stood naked in the candlelight as the doctor, with another candle, searched their bodies, dropping hot wax in quite sensitive places.

'Rheumatic fever, where did you get that?' Edward asked a man in his twenties.

'In the army, Doctor,' the man replied.

'I'll pass you for the Club; you are good for a few years yet.'

As the doctor treated his patients, took temperatures, examined tongues and eyelids, listened to the throbbing of hearts with his stethoscope, Violet stood in the road waiting for emergencies, an early ambulance of sorts. Violet was harnessed every morning by the doctor's manservant, and the trap stood all day long with Violet between the shafts eating from a nosebag.

A vivid picture of his son, Edward Buckram Overthrow, flaxen-haired and Norfolk-jacketed, driving the doctor to the station in a high trap brings back a thrill difficult to explain. The doctor was always late, he rarely left before the train was coming out of the next station two miles away. Then, with his son driving, he came at full gallop past our house, his son shouting, 'Violet, Violet, you wasted life. Do you think I stole you?' Sometimes the train would be leaving the station and would wait for him along by the sidings.

Dr Overthrow was an excellent shot. He loved his gun and his spaniel dog, and rented a shoot on the sixty acres adjoining Ashton Wood on the slopes of Bredon Hill.

What other doctor took his gun to visit his patients on his rounds, I wonder. My cousin George was ill with 'flu. The doctor arrived and, not waiting for an answer to his knock, walked straight in. George, who was sitting by his fireside, was confronted by the doctor carrying his gun. He looked up from his chair and, still feeling pretty low, said, 'You haven't come to shoot me Doctor?'

The old doctor's deafness caused many a laugh. 'How are you, boy, I brought you into the world over twenty years ago.'

George replied, 'Oh, I'm better, but have a nasty boil on my neck.'

'Let your trousers down,' the doctor said, propping his gun in the corner of George's cottage sitting-room.

'My neck, Doctor, MY NECK!' shouted George.

'Ah, a bread poultice with a little salt, as hot as you can bear it and I'll give you a tonic. You are run down my lad.' The doctor then walked home under the wood, not empty-handed for his gun kept the family in rabbits and game throughout the season.

In 1890 when Dr Overthrow first came to live in the village, the nearest doctor was six miles away, and he soon had a number of patients all around Bredon Hill. Village folk are slow to accept 'outsiders', but when I was a boy the doctor was part of the village scene. However, with the exception of Millie Bostock, he was never accepted by the Bostock family. This hostility arose partly from the doctor's marriage to Amy, Millie's sister, when he was nearly fifty and almost twice her age. William Henry, the Squire, a close relative of Amy's, had been fabulously rich, but had squandered his fortune in the markets and fairs as his mental state became progressively worse. He thought that Edward was marrying young Amy for a stake in the Bostock fortune, and he once offered my Uncle Jim one hundred sovereigns to shoot the doctor. Further fury was aroused when the doctor had tried to save some of the arthritic elderly men from having to work for the Squire. They stood ankle deep in ditches, hedging and ditching and draining the Squire's land. 'I have had the best out of you and now I'll have the worst,' the Squire often said.

Squire Bostock, although a member of the School Board, took much less interest than the doctor in the comings and goings at the school where the temperature was often low. The times the doctor had walked down the road with his thermometer! He passed between the rows of children looking for signs of measles, scarlet fever, in fact, looking for anything that their parents had overlooked. The doctor was indeed a great asset to the village of Ashton.

The doctor, it's quite evident, was always concerned for the poor. They trusted him when their babies were born. There was a case of a premature birth when the child was thought to be dead; this was at a time before intensive care and incubators. The doctor worked on the child and it began to breathe and cry. He dabbed a little brandy on its lips. It lived and as the boy grew to manhood, he called it the miracle baby.

Edward Overthrow sought no reward for the long hours he spent in all winds and weathers at night-time, while the village lay sleeping on their feather mattresses. Honour, the widow of a railway ganger, lay between life and death fighting pneumonia. It was late on a Sunday night when the doctor called.

'No crisis, yet, but she needs poulticing,' he told Tom Wheatcroft, her son. 'And I'm run out of linseed meal.' Tom said, 'Doctor, there's plenty of linseed over in the barn which I use for the calves, but it's not been ground into meal.'

'Damn it, we can grind it can't we,' the doctor replied. 'Do half a hundredweight Tom, there's a hell of a lot of 'flu about and other people will go down with it and need poulticing.'

The doctor stayed to poultice the old woman every two hours, saying, 'These small hours are the worst for pneumonia patients.' He and Tom talked the night away, drinking cider, one each side of the range; two experts discussing the diseases and treatment of people and animals. Honour survived the crisis and lived until she was eighty-five.

Blenheim once told me, 'Old Dr Overthrow did operations just arter that one on King Edud (for appendicitis). Skilful man with the knife was our doctor and I'm a gwain to tell tha summat now as thee mindust not swallow. Boy, it's as true as this ash plant's in my hand. Dr Overthrow operated on pigs at the bacon factory in A'sum (Evesham), just to get his hand in afore he started on humans; now whether a pig a got an appendix or no I can't tell ya.'

A man for his time, Edward Overthrow watched no clock but the sun and the moon, out with his gun in the day and visiting at all hours during the night.

He often operated on dining-tables. In one case, a pregnancy in the fallopian tubes was terminated on a dining-table in one of the big houses. She was a poor girl who fell foul of a chauffeur.

Confinements were commonplace, but Edward would be there at any time, helped by Betsy Bradfield who was a partly trained midwife and a layer-out of the dead. He had an inimitable humour. Mrs J. who lived up Bakers Lane in a thatched cottage, the wife of a carter, had three daughters and so badly wanted a son. When the doctor was delivering the baby, 'What is it Doctor?' she anxiously asked.

'Wait a bit Ellen, a little longer. Ah, it's another girl.'

Ellen burst into tears sobbing her heart out and crying, 'Doctor, I did so much want a boy.'

He knew Ellen and spoke to her not as some out-of-touch medico, but as a friend, a village anchor, and a man who understood the small world under the hill. 'It's no good Ellen, not your fault at all, but Old Jack can't get you a baby with a spout on. Perhaps you ought to try a different horse.' Here was language that the carter's wife understood; kind in a way, the doctor was trying to make light of Ellen's plight. Her tears dried and she laughed.

I do remember Mrs Amy Overthrow. As a small boy I saw her often sitting on a chair underneath the pear tree opposite Rockland House. She was by then an invalid, looked after by her daughters. Her death in middle age was a great blow to her husband. She had, despite indifferent health, steered the Overthrow ship as a young mother.

When Amy died, her eldest daughter Mary never again went out of doors in the day, remaining for nearly sixty-five years a recluse in Rockland House, only paying visits to her family and friends at night. The doctor, an old man with a young family, took little notice of his children's education, and the two sons became small yeoman farmers, Buckram of course was the Midnight Milkman.

The youngest daughter was so beautiful that she stood out in a village where plainness was the rule. Dressed in the height of fashion (her more serious brother was shocked at the shortness of her skirts) she was driven about by suitors with motor cars, at a time when cars were a rarity, one to a village like parish churches. One young man's Morris Cowley was pushed into Carrants Brook by a jealous rival.

One Christmas at Rockland House, the doctor was missing after supper, much to the consternation of the family, for several times that winter he had suffered heart attacks. On his return, he said, 'I've been to mark my grave under the yew tree. I've sold my surgical instruments to young Savery. He says that with wooden handles to my knives they can't be sterilised and the instruments are going to a museum.'

Soon after this, my brother and I, on holiday from school, were going to the shop to buy sweets when we heard someone calling for help. The call came from the orchard of Rockland House and we found the doctor lying on the grass beside a five-barred gate. It appeared that he had fallen when he opened the gate. We held the doctor's arms and lifted him on to his feet. He wasn't a big man. He was breathing heavily but we managed to help him into the house. 'Are you Tom Archer's boys?' he asked.

'Yes', we answered.

'I shall write to Tom Archer and tell him how you helped me.'

He died soon after this and Barbara, his third daughter, arranged the funeral at the church. Millie Bostock played the organ. Edward Overthrow's death left a gap in the village community which could never be filled. It's true he hadn't been very active during his last years but he was always there at Rockland House, as he had been for so long. There to advise and comfort the old village families, and the children he had brought into the world. Although in many ways a controversial figure, he was almost worshipped by the old folk.

6

Work

For centuries, farming had depended on the power of man and beast. I knew and worked with men who remembered the age-old methods. Old Shepherd Corbisley told me of driving bullocks at plough on the Cotswolds as a boy, and how they used to make the bullock run away with the plough by putting a bree fly by the bullock's ear. Our ancient Cross Barn had its threshing floor, and Walt told me that he first used the flail in that barn. 'We was a-threshing beans, me and old Josey Summers. Now when you stands opposite and works together you brings your hinged stick down in turn. Well, ya see,' he says, 'I got sort of out of step with old Josey and ketched him the master smack with my flail on the top of his yud. My boy, didn't he tell me my fortune!' Josey was laid to rest years after under the churchyard wall. Walt died in 1969 aged 87; the flails are just museum pieces.

Well before the end of the nineteenth century, however, the arrival of steampower had brought its noisy contribution to the mechanisation of farming. The huge steam-ploughing machines had only been used on the biggest farms, but the threshing machine had come to stay. Threshing the corn was a winter job, and took at least seven men and boys. The steam engine, machine and straw tier came over from Winchcombe, and we started our sweaty, dusty day of seemingly endless toil at seven the next morning. All day long the sheaves were fed into the machine, the sacks of grain were wheeled into the granary and the boltings of straw were moved from the straw tier to build a straw rick. My tasks were to carry the chaff into the barn, to keep the water butt full for the steam engine and to help the shepherd build the straw rick. At dusk, the rats began to run out of the last sheaves left in the Dutch barn, to be killed by boys with sticks and terriers. As night fell, the machine slowed down and then stopped, bringing a sudden welcome silence.

The first Fordson tractor, fuelled by paraffin, arrived on Stanley Farm in the mid–1920s, but did not unsurp the horse teams pulling the seed-drills, ploughs and harrows. Horses could work in wet, heavy clay and were not

Steam ploughing

Steam threshing

subject to mechanical breakdowns. But, just as the silent scythe had been replaced by the clattering of the mowing machine, the whack of the flail by the din of the threshing machine, the tractor was a harbinger of the changes that would overtake the farming techniques which I knew as a boy.

THE PARTNERS

My father, Tom Archer, and Harry Carter were partners, market gardening and farming nearly five hundred acres. Mr Carter, who had come from Evesham, was the expert in market gardening. He knew everything there was to know of the growing and marketing of peas, sprouts, beans, plums and strawberries. Dad, ten years younger, knew how to assess and buy the right cattle for fattening; as a boy he had learnt to plough and to shear, to drench ewes and calves.

Mr Carter was impulsive and could get up in the boughs when roused by incompetence or dishonesty, but he had the ability to forgive and forget very soon. Dad was quiet, steady and afraid of no one. He was a worrier, a solver of sums, a planner of crops.

On market days, Mr Carter dressed in grey tweed breeches, cloth gaiters, light black boots he called his tea-drinkers, a tweed jacket, fancy waistcoat, starched shirt and grey trilby hat. Dad wore a brown tweed suit, brown chrome boots, lightly nailed, and his soft white collar and spotted tie gave a finish to his Oxford shirt. His check cap gave the impression that he was about to go to a point-to-point, but neither he nor Harry had time for such luxuries. They did go to a lot of farm sales, though, for they bought all their equipment and machinery second-hand, the only exception I can remember being the Greens hayloader.

Their workaday clothes were somewhat different. They rarely wore a jacket winter or summer, but could be seen stripped to the shirt working with their men on the land.

There is one more thing these two diverse characters had in common. Working the land, planting, harvesting, making the hay, weighing the peas, they always took their guns, were always accompanied by their dogs – Dad's a liver and white spaniel, Mr Carter's an Italian greyhound. Dogs and guns lay on the headland of the field while their masters worked. It's hard to say which man was the better shot. Tom would down the passing pigeon as it sailed high above the hedgerow elms. Mr Carter planted parsley on Bredon Hill to attract the hares. He had an eye like a hawk and I have never seen rabbits bowled over running as he did it, with his twelve-bore gun inches in front of his dog's nose. I lost his best fitcher ferret deep in a holt in Clay Furlong. 'Never mind, boy, you'll learn,' he said. 'You cut the line, I suppose.' I had to admit I did. 'Don't forget to tell your Dad what a hard day's rabbiting we've had today,' he said. We had been digging in rock but we had a good bag. Lately it has dawned on me why Mr Carter liked my company. He hadn't a son of his own.

Dad's and Mr Carter's methods wouldn't do today but they made an impact on this village.

THE SPROUTS TAKE OVER

All the old farmers I ever met said it was Lloyd George who let them down after the 1914 war. Somebody had to take the blame and in the early twenties everything slumped in price, especially corn. Some farmers just let their land tumble down to grass, not having the spirit to sow leys (pasture); others went in for market gardening. This industry had been mostly

Mr Harry Carter with his wife, family and friends outside Old Manor Farm

confined to the Evesham Vale, good early land, but sprouts and peas grew quite well in our village and some farmers grew a fair acreage of sprouts, others let fields to the more experienced Evesham growers. Dad and his partner were one step ahead of the local farmers; they had been growing sprouts and other market crops in a big way since about 1907. They had developed an excellent strain of brussels sprouts by selecting stems of their own and growing their own seed on top of Bredon Hill, miles away from any other green stuff, which was important to prevent cross fertilisation by bees. Archer and Carter's strain was locally famous. Where you have a good article and a good name in the market, good workmen are a must. Both Dad and Mr Carter were most particular about the growing and picking of sprouts; the plants had to be firm, the ground had to be just right.

Before I left school I had seen, so often, Mr Carter and Dad pulling a wooden hand-marker to mark out the rows for the sprout plants. Just a wooden frame with legs formed by the rounds, or rungs, from an old ladder. In those days sprouts were planted three feet between the rows, but the distance between the plants varied according to the man with the setting pins or dibber.

The local sprout growers had a good ally in Tom Harris of Sedgeberrow. Tom was a blacksmith with an inventive mind. A suggestion from a grower and Tom would make anything.

He modified the steerage horse-hoe, which had a tool bar where the legs and shears could be adjusted according to the width between the rows of the crop. Tom made a long tool bar to replace the usual one for marking out. Five legs it had, fixed with collars and set screws, so by placing these three feet apart and running the one leg down the last mark, four marks could be made for sprout planting.

This led to a change of pattern in sprout growing. By marking a field lengthways, and crossways, and planting the sprouts where the lines met, the sprouts could be skimmed or horse-hoed both ways. This saved a lot of work, because the only part left for hand-hoeing was the small square of ground around the plant where the skim didn't cut the weeds.

Every plant was firmed by the setting pin and tested by pulling at the leaf with finger and thumb to prove when the leaf tore away that the plant was firm in the soil. A teaspoonful of sulphate of ammonia was put close to each plant when the plants started growing; close to each plant meant that the backs of the men were bent double as the white sugary sulphate was dribbled through the hand almost touching the ground. If the fertiliser fell on the plant it scorched it, and if it fell a foot away the fibrous roots of the plant could not reach it.

After a day of up and down every yard, the spine numbed. The only relief, as the summer sun warmed the labourers at bait time (lunch), was to take half an hour lying flat on the grassy headland.

The ploughing of Quar Hill by the partners in the early 1930s for sprouts was a turning point in the working of the land. Until then it was the accepted thing, a practice no one questioned, that Walt mowed the brookside Hams first. The milking cows grazed Tun Flun, the horses Boss Close and Shepherd Corbisley lambed his ewes in Church Close. All permanent pasture. It takes a lifetime to make a good permanent ley, the old men said. The same thing applied to the plough land. Finches Piece grew the mangolds. I suspect this was because when the muck was carted from the cattle yards, this was the nearest arable field. So every year in early winter, the muck heaps in Finches Piece stood in rows like brown pitched tents ready for the spreading. Then the field was ploughed before Christmas. Cabbages grew year after year along Beckfords Way. The chickweed, like green mats, was horse-hoed, hand-hoed and never grew less. Peas grew in Hempits, where the nearby ditch turned the twigs into stone, a marvel to me in those days. Here coltsfoot smothered the land, and scarlet pimpernel and groundsel competed with the peas. When the peas were clear of weeds by man power and horse power, sprouts were planted between the rows. It was always the same pattern; the old order never seemed to change until despite the limestone rock the sprouts grew on Quar Hill.

MY FIRST HORSE-HOEING

I was nine when Dad took me horse-hoeing for the first time in Carrants Field. In the nag stable, formerly used for hunters, Dad put the gears, or harness, on Tom the nag.

I noticed that the seventeen-hand cart-horses, heavy legged with feathers covering their great hooves, wore different collars from Tom. Their linings were check patterned like a bookie's jacket; Tom's was navy like Dad's Sunday suit.

For horse-hoeing the usual harness was a set of GO gear, a light type of chain harness. Hames, back band and light traces with small links. It differed from the ordinary long gears carried by the plough team. No crupper, no hip straps.

Dad and Mr Carter never missed a local farm sale. It was a social occasion. They bought ex-WD harnesses which were used to pull the guns by horses in the 1914–18 war. The traces we used on the nag were of wire cable neatly covered with leather. Light yet strong, and the hooks could be strapped in such a way that they never came undone when turning on the headland. Absolutely ideal for horse-hoeing.

'It's about time you made a start, Fred. I thought you couldn't go wrong among the sprouts.' Dad carried a short stick in one hand, with binder twine hanging from it which made it look like a small whip.

'What's that for, Dad?' I asked.

'You will see presently.'

The morning hedges were drenched with dew. The sun was up but at a quarter past seven it had not dried the sprouts in Carrants Field. With buckled leggings over my three-quarter-length school stockings I slid off the nag's back. The sprouts were above knee-high to me.

'They will soon dry,' Dad said, 'when the sun gets a bit higher. But meanwhile I don't want to get you wet through.' He then tied some sacking above my leggings to keep my knees dry.

'Now the stick,' he said. 'If I tie this on Tom's mullin (bridle) by the bit, you can guide Tom up one row and walk up the next, holding the end of the stick, and when I say off a bit, push his head up.'

'What about when you want to keep to the left, Dad?' I asked.

'Oh, then I'll say, "To you a bit".'

I'll never forget that first horse-hoeing with Dad and the nag in Carrants Field. When the dew had dried off the sprouts by ten o'clock, we sat under the hedge and had our lunch. There was really no need for Dad to look at his watch to time us for half an hour. The train to Birmingham passed the level crossing at a quarter to ten and that meant about two more bouts, or twice up the field and twice back and then it would be lunch-time. A light engine, as the locals called it, passed at the appropriate time to return to work. Then the sacking came off my knees and I felt free to walk the long alley of sprouts while Dad held the tails or handles of the horse-hoe.

On the headland as I led Tom into the next row I realised that the stick on the bridle not only made it easier for me to reach and control his bitted mouth but it also enabled me to walk that little distance from those iron-shod hooves of his. Many a boy has gone home with blackened toenails where the keenness of the pulling horse with his iron-shod fore-feet has sunk some little boot into the clay.

The length of the day! At every bout, that is, every time we reached the headland near the railroad, Dad lightly spat on his hands as he gripped the horse-hoe tails and quietly said, 'Cup, boy.' Tom walked a steady pace all day. The monotony of rows of sprouts standing in the summer sun like lines of little trees made me turn at each end with a sort of instinct. About twice, apart from meal times, we stopped and swigged Eiffel Tower lemonade from a pint-and-a-half bottle. I saw the young thistles we had cut with the share earlier in the day wilting in the sun as I fetched the bottle, and I picked a few loganberries off a bush in the hedge on the way back. But the five-twenty train eventually came, the little tank engine pulling her three coaches Birmingham way, and Dad undid the traces and left the horse-hoe on the headland.

'Legs ache, Fred boy?' asked Dad. He knew they did and, he gave me a leg up on to Tom's back. 'I'll walk across Tun Flun. You take the horse around up the lane.'

Tom knew his way up the back lane and one dig in the ribs and he trotted, jolting me. I gripped the hames and what a relief from the endless track of walking the avenues of sprouts in Carrants Field.

Dad was waiting at the stable door and he showed me how to undo the harness, hang up the gear and hold Tom by his forelock as he turned the collar with its sweat-stained lining and after undoing the chin-strap, slipped the mullin over his head. The last thing I noticed Tom lose was the bit from his dusty mouth which had kept him straight all day.

Dad brushed the tide mark of sweat off the nag's shoulders and then we let him loose. Away he galloped up the orchard and rolled over and over on his back under the trees before he trotted through the open gate into Boss Close.

I thought it was lucky for me that Dad broke me into the secrets of leading a horse instead of putting me at the mercy of some clod-throwing carter.

THE SPROUT-PICKING CHAMPIONSHIP

Picking sprouts has changed a lot since those days. The old pickers packed forty pounds into the bags or wicker hampers; then, in the twenties, Mr Robert Cambridge invented the sprout net to hold twenty pounds. He bought second-hand fish netting from Lowestoft, the women in his packing-shed cut this into squares and a cottage industry developed in our village as both men and women wove these squares of netting with soft string into net containers. The advantages of the net were that the sprouts could be seen by the buyer, they kept in good condition with plenty of air and they looked much more of an attractive pack than a forty-pound

George, the sprout-picking champion, with Tom Archer on the left and Mr Cartwright, from Harveys of Kidderminster who provided the fertilizer, on the right

hamper. The industry continued for a while until it was taken over by the fish netting manufacturers.

We had several pickers who could pick sixty nets a day piece work, but George Hampton, Oliver's nephew, was the Maestro. He had long fingers, a strong wrist and with his fingers moving all the time he was easily the fastest sprout-picker in the district.

George was also a clean picker, all the yellow leaves and bits of stem slipped through his fingers and fell to the ground and the hard button sprouts dropped into the nets. His nets filled with remarkable speed and every so often one of George's clenched fists pushed the sprouts down into the very corners of the nets and made the pack easy to see and much more attractive to look at. It's hard to work up much enthusiasm about sprout picking; conditions are wet, cold and frosty at that time of the year and a field of sprouts with white hoar frost covering it does not look very inviting at seven-thirty on a winter's day.

One January we had a piece of sprouts on some land rented for the year from a local farmer who had done the ground well, sheeping off turnips the year before. Dad and Mr Carter gave it a good supply of meat and bone manure and the crop of sprouts was a sight for sore eyes. George started with the rest of the gang picking sprouts into twenty-pound nets as soon as the morning sun peeped over Broadway Hill. Tom Harris, the Sedgeberrow blacksmith, had perfected a sprout net holder – just a simple crate with hooks at each of the four top corners. He and Mr Cambridge made this especially to take a sprout net stretched wide open for filling. George kept a supply of empty nets under the belt of his coat and as he filled them he left them in a neat row between the sprout stems. Dad came for dinner at one o'clock, and said, 'I believe George is going to make history today. I reckon he won't be far short of picking eighty nets by dark at half past four.'

About a quarter to five Dad drove the Sunbeam tourer into the yard. He had just helped to load the last of the sprouts after they had been weighed on the spring balance hung from a rough tripod of nut sticks on the headland. As he washed in cold water in our kitchen sink, he said, 'Well, young George have done it – eighty nets in under eight hours.'

The news went round the village. Some old stagers said it couldn't be done. 'He never carried um out and weighed um,' said others, but George did all that and picked them clean. The local paper got to know about it and under the title 'Is this a Record?' published an article about George. Letters poured in. Some pickers said, 'Oi, and the gaffer ul expect us all to do it every day and piece-work rates will go down,' but nothing like that happened. There was only one George – I've picked with him and worked hard for forty nets in a day, while George had got sixty by three o'clock.

Some of the Evesham gardeners who were jealous of their skill at growing vegetables said, 'Let's have a competition and see who can pick the most sprouts, picked cleanly, in two hours.' The following year a competition was held in a large field near Pershore. Publicity was given to this in the local and national press. The BBC sent Robin Whitworth down to report; even Beachcomber mentioned it in his column. Cameramen came to film it for the cinemas and a silver cup was given by the firm who supplied us with the fertiliser. 'It's all a stunt,' some of the A'sum (Evesham) crowd said. 'Just to sell Tom Archer's and Harry Carter's sprout sid. Did'st see it advertised in the *Journal*? – twenty shillings a pound mind tha.' We had two wheat sacks full of seed standing both sides of the oven grate in our kitchen and it was now part of my duties to weigh it into pounds and post it to all parts of the country.

I went over to see the competition early in Mr Carter's car with Dad and George. It was a bitter cold morning in mid-winter. Picking started at ten thirty and lasted until twelve thirty; at nine o'clock when we arrived on the field, the sprouts were dropping their leaves with frost and a fog lay over the Vale. We had some lunch and a hot flask of tea and the sun broke through, partly thawing the rime on the sprout leaves. George was like a boxer before the fight, he hopped about from one foot to the other and was raring to go.

By now the pickers were lined up like athletes about to run a race. Two rows of sprouts each, and behind every picker an important man with 'Steward' printed on a yellow disc fixed to the lapel of his coat. The stewards followed four yards behind each picker. If a picker did not clear all the sprouts off each stem, the steward fetched him back to do so. The steward had also to see that no sprouts were thrown on the ground and that no leaves or bits of stem were put in the nets.

George took off his overcoat and then, to our amazement on this bitter cold morning when we had turned-up collars and scarves, he took off his jacket too and hung both on the hawthorn hedge on the headland; there he stood rolling up his sleeves, waistcoated, on that winter day, his large hands trembling a little until the whistle was blown to start the competition. Within minutes George had filled his first net.

The pickers, backs bent, worked down the long field like an army advancing. It was fairly quiet apart from the rustling of the sprout leaves and the cracking of the sprouts as they were pushed off the stems by the palm of the hand. Occasionally we heard a steward fetch back a picker to clear a stem but these men were what was known as everyday sprouters and needed little supervision. After two hours the whistle blew, the sprouts were weighed and each picker had at least one of his nets emptied out onto an empty dray for the judges to scrutinise, looking for leaves and bits of stem and judging the quality of the pack. One man was disqualified for rough picking and George, as we had hoped, won the cup; he picked the most and picked them clean and proved to everyone that he did pick eighty nets in under eight hours the previous January. The cup was presented at a little function in Evesham Town Hall and George broadcast to the nation how to pick sprouts.

Since this great day in the little world of sprout-pickers, men have topped the hundred mark, picking over one hundred nets in a day; new varieties have been introduced, but in their day Archer and Carter's strain stood supreme.

At the Regal Cinema at Evesham on the Saturday afternoon, we saw George in the newsreel picking sprouts, the King of Sprout-pickers from Ashton.

HAYMAKING

The number of people who quenched their thirst with a pint-and-a-half bottle of Aunty Phoebe's pop for twopence will never be known. It was good heady stuff made from some ancient recipe and was at its best when it was about a week old. We thrived on it in the June hayfields.

The sorts and shapes of her bottles varied from square-shaped coffee-essence bottles to long wine bottles which Tom Wheatcroft kept because they had a long neck for drenching cows. Aunty Phoebe kept a little sweet shop in the front room of her thatched cottage, where she also sold her home-made raspberry vinegar and mushroom ketchup, but pop was her best-seller during the summer. She brewed this in a copper furnace and when she had bottled it all the corks, which had a slit across the top, were tied in with pudding string. If we just wanted a glass this was a penny. It was stone cold and refreshing.

Oliver took a bottle of pop with him to work in the summer and for weeks on end kept off the cider. Oliver never dabbled in anything and when he had what he called a session, it was serious. There was a special quart cup kept for him at the pub. A pint would have been an insult. For a few days he would be backwards and forwards past our house and once more he would have broken his resolution not to have another spot of cider.

When he returned to work after a few days of heavy drinking Tom Wheatcroft described him as 'conterairy'. Oliver often loaded the waggons and if every pitchforkful of hay wasn't placed on the waggon by the pitchers exactly where Oliver wanted it, he complained. This soon wore off and Oliver was back to his usual genial mood.

Tom and Walt were our best hay pitchers and Oliver and Shepherd Corbisley were a well-matched pair loading the waggons. But when the shepherd was wanted as rick builder Taffy, the blue-eyed, fair-haired Welshman, helped Oliver to build the loads. He, like so many of his day, had arrived by road with his little bundle and stayed in the harness room next to the nag stable where there was a fireplace; he was there for years. He was one of the few roadsters that I was a bit afraid of. I remember he threatened to put the prongs of a hay fork through a youth of my age on the farm. But he amused us with some of his tales of farming on the Welsh hills. Tales of sheep stealing were amusing at lunch-times, but after he had told us how several of his companions murdered the shepherd on the Black Mountains we were careful not to cross him.

Haymaking, as I like to recall it, was at Great Hill on Bredon when the sainfoin rick was built. Sainfoin is a Cotswold clover rather similar to lucerne but with a red flower which blooms early. This twenty-five-ton rick was built in the same place every year handy to the barn, on a straw staddle or foundation. Walt mowed the Peewit Hill and as the sainfoin wilted I had old Captain in a primitive swathe turner and turned the swathes. Captain only had one speed – dead slow; and Tom Wheatcroft jokingly got behind a larch tree up there and I asked him what he was doing. 'Just a-seeing if thee wast a-moving.'

Summer-time on Bredon meant the smell of the new-mown sainfoin, the circling peewits, the larks ascending. When Frank Davis and I horse-raked the hay into walleys I was allowed Bonnie and he the more agile Pleasant. We had to get the rows of hay in the walley fairly straight because, if it worked, the Greens hayloader was used to pick up the hay. This was the only machine which the partners bought new, and it was always breaking down. This was hitched to the back of the waggon and two younger men loaded it. With three horses snatching at the traces, the loaders had to be sure-footed when Walt and I or Frank led the team, straddling the walleys or rows of hay. When the loaders got 'mowed up' or had too much hay coming up into the waggon they shouted 'Whoa'. It was then difficult to start a nearly loaded waggon with this loader behind without the horses snatching. 'Hold tight,' shouted Walt. I held Turpin, the foremost, under his chin, tightening the bit in his mouth from both sides of his 'mullin' or bridle acting like the choke chain on a dog. If, by Turpin snatching, one of our loaders had been pitched off, Dad or Mr Carter might have sent me scaring birds off the peas, and I wanted to be among the hay. Dinner-time in the hayfield miles from anywhere, the horses pulling their well-deserved meal from the back of a loaded waggon, and then a half-mile trek with them to the stone trough on Furze Hill to water them, can never be erased from the memory.

Then as about fourteen men and boys sat down in the shade of the beech trees and listened to the wisdom of these older men, who were the salt of the earth, Frank and Geoff and I, all boys, just drank in the stories of poaching from Oliver and of hay as it should be made from the shepherd. Mr Carter told us of harvesting all day with two hooks and how his small brother forgot to bring him his dinner and he worked until dark 'not having bit nor spot all day'. Then he told us about Joseph Arch speaking to them from a farm waggon about joining the Workers' Union. 'It was old Lloyd George who give us the pension,' the old shepherd said. 'See what they have done to Elliot,' (then Minister of Agriculture) he went on. 'Throwed eggs and tomaters at him and he'll get wo'se than that 'it.'

My small tin of sardines for dinner nearly brought tears to my eyes when

A break for dinner among the hay. Note the cider barrel

the key broke. Dear old Uncle George opened them with his pocket knife. Besides Aunty Phoebe's pop, Uncle had a flask of tea. This was the first vacuum flask I saw and he poured a cupful into *The Daily Chronicle* of the day before, for his spaniel, Tiny, to drink with a little condensed milk. If Dad and Mr Carter were there (they usually were) we had just the hour for dinner. When Uncle was in charge he'd get up at two o'clock, dead on time, and pulling out his watch, came out with his usual, 'I do believe if I didn't make a move you jumping byoys'd stop here all day.' Frank and I had cheap watches and would say, 'It wants another two minutes to two.' Uncle, whose watch could be relied on like Big Ben, said, 'Mine was right by Beech's hooter (at the jam factory) at eight o'clock this morning and I'll tell ya what it is, you can't do too much for a good master.' 'Poor old Uncle's got past it,' one of us would say. 'Yes, and you chaps a fellas ant got to it yet.' We teased him but he bore no malice.

After dinner the shepherd, Dad and Tom Wheatcroft started making the staddle or rick bottom from some straw Walt had brought up and the waggons were unloaded, first by hand, until the rick reached about eight feet high. Then came the moment everyone had been expecting, the raising of the monkey pole. These poles were in two sections, jointed like a fishing rod, and were used to elevate the hay from the waggon on to the rick. To raise the pole upright, half a load of hay was left on the waggon and the pole lifted on the waggon, the top at an angle over the shaft horse's head and the butt end secured by two iron spikes driven through two rings into the ground. Dad stood on the waggon and as Walt backed the filler or shaft horse the pole became more upright. Fixed to the top of the pole on a swivel were four guy ropes. A man held each one of these as the pole became almost vertical. Dad gave out his orders quietly, 'Hang on to yours, Tom. Let yours go a bit, George. Come round a bit, Taffy.' Oliver then drove long iron spikes into the ground with a sledge-hammer. These had T pieces on the top; the guy ropes were tied to them and we breathed again. A steady shaft horse like Captain was vital.

A pulley wheel at the foot of the pole was for a rope which passed through two pulleys on the crane-like jib and was fastened to two enormous forks like grappling irons, sharp, three-pronged and heavy. Captain was hitched to the end of the rope on the ground alongside the rick, and when the forks or grabs were shoved into the hay on the waggon a good forkful was raised off it as Captain moved a few yards forward. The jib swung across and over the rick, the unloader on the waggon pulled a trip cord and the hay fell in a heap in the rick. Captain then had to be backed to give enough slack rope for the forks to be again pushed into the hay on the waggon. As I led Captain to and fro, Jack Bradfield unloaded, and by keeping my eyes open I enabled things to work like clockwork. But Captain had a very hard mouth and he took some backing. He would see-saw at his bit and if Walt was unloading and getting a bit impatient, he'd shout, 'Let's have a bit more pudding. This don't half give my arms summat.'

'How's that corner of the rick, Fred?' Tom Wheatcroft, who was building it, would shout. 'Put it out about a foot,' I'd say, if I thought he was drawing it in, but he came off the rick every load to see if we were going on all right.

When Tom went to suckle the calves, milk the house cow and feed the weaned calves at four o'clock, the shepherd took over building the rick, but when I got to be about twelve years old Dad would send me down off the hill because Tom couldn't be spared. I got the milking cows in out of Tun Flun, tied them up in the long shed and let the calves out of their pens to suck them. Old Grannie was the house cow and it was like getting blood out of a stone to milk her. Her own calf had what was left and as Tom didn't want him to make a pig of himself he gave me instructions to 'Mind and get a bucketful out of old Grannie afore you let that calf suck.' I could just

Building a hayrick on the river meadows at Bredon

about handle her great teats in my small hands and as I sat on that greasy old three-legged stool with my cap on back to front I wrested half a bucketful from Grannie. She was unwilling to let it down; she wanted to keep it for her calf.

When I got back to the hayfield the rick was three parts built, and Dad and Mr Carter had been looking at some hay Walt had cut two days before. Mr Carter's crystal set predicted rain and Dad said, 'We'll turn it again and pick it up before night and finish the rick.' The shepherd said, 'It's never fit in this wide world. You'll have it fire as safe as eggs. Rain! It won't rain, the wind w'ere tis.' It was picked up a bit green, or 'gay' as Tom said. It didn't fire, but the top of the rick got warm and was a brown colour and smelt of tobacco when Tom cut it in the winter for his store cattle. The shepherd had some of the better sainfoin out of the bottom for his ewes. Even that wasn't just right. The horse rakes had knocked all the leaf off it. 'No herbage,' he said. He lived to see some cut and made with the tractor but told me. 'Them ship won't yut it; it stinks o' paraffin.'

We had to turn an oatrick once because it got hot. The heat was sore on the feet as we turned the sheaves and Tom told the old shepherd we had 'lost a gold watch in the rick and was trying to find him'.

Haymaking memories are happy ones. Saturday night Dad and Mr Carter would get all the vehicles they could lay their hands on and all went pitching and loading hay as Walt brought them up to our rickyard. The first load drew up to the rick, the next close behind, and I have seen eight or nine waggons loaded on Saturday nights with their middle well filled in case of a wet weekend, the last waggon almost in the road. And there was something to start with on Monday morning, unloading first the borrowed waggons, then our own five. The hay from the Dewnests and Thurness had to be hauled over the station bridge and as I had the leading rein on the foremost and Walt led the filler we cantered over the bridge. The loads were well roped. I can picture the men of those days roping loads, hitching the rope to the hooks on the side of the waggon and coming out with showers of hay seeds gone down under their shirts. I can see now the old panama hats, the billycock hats, battered trilbies and cloth caps; the broad braces of the men, whose noses dripped with sweat as they worked to save a valuable winter feed. (I knew only one man who went hatless, winter and summer, the bald driver of the threshing machine.) Waistcoats, shirts and flannel undershirts were never removed, however hot the sun. The women wore white bonnets, with a frill which kept the sun off the nape of the neck, and sacking aprons.

The wage was sevenpence farthing an hour and ninepence an hour overtime. Mr Carter and Dad never advertised for labour. They both knew what a good day's work was and working with them got it from the men. There were two masters but they spoke as one and were more eager to encourage than to criticise. Both master and man made hay while the sun shone and took it a little steadier as the rain took over, hoping that the next day the sun might be shining.

EWES, RAMS AND LAMBS

At the end of every September both the partners went up into mid-Wales to buy some fresh Kerry ewes. These came by rail to Beckford Station about two miles away. I usually went with the shepherd and his dog Rosie to meet the train and drive the ewes home. As they came out of the truck he would watch them with a critical eye as the little puffs of blue smoke from his clay pipe rose into the fine September afternoon. 'They a bought a wrung un thur, Fred. Lumpy jaw.' As the ewes, glad to get out of the trucks, nibbled

Both master and man made hay while the sun shone and took it a little steadier as the rain took over, hoping that the next day the sun might be shining.

'My poor old aunt at Nottingham has passed away,' Kate Dunn
told Millie and was overheard by Jimmy Blizzard who remarked,
'thur's a funny thing, passed away, my relations allus died.'

Shepherd Corbisley with a flock of ewes on Bredon Hill

at the bit of grass in the station yard, the shepherd sized them up. 'They beunt a bad bunch, take um on the whole.' Catching one with his crook he would open its mouth with the gentleness and manner of a dentist. 'That un a got six tith so hers three.' In those days ewes were 'got-up for sale', that is, they were coloured with a yellow ochre. The shepherd told me, 'It's supposed to make um look bigger but it don't.' We moved the new flock very slowly. I walked in front, the shepherd and his dog behind. 'They ull soon want some water so we'll put them in the first ham by Carrants Brook.' Shutting the gate, the shepherd and I walked about another half a mile home, when he told me all the good and bad points about his new charges. 'Thur's one or two of um, Fred, as looks as if they bin getting through the fences. They be craw-necked.' He meant they had lost some wool off their necks. 'They beunt bad on thur fit. Only one lame and that ull be put right tomorrow. What we wants now is four good tups (rams) to put with them. I suppose yer Dad and Mr Carter will be off to Gloucester, to Barton Fair on the 29th?'

I said, 'Yes. I am going with them on the train.'

On the 29th Shepherd Corbisley was waiting on the platform with Bert, who had brought him down with Min in the milk float. The rams were loaded into the float under the shepherd's critical eye. 'Four smartish rams, Master,' the shepherd said, 'although I beunt all that keen on the one marked No 3.'

'Why,' Mr Carter said, 'he's a good long ram.'

'Oi, I knows all about that but thur's too much daylight under him.' What he meant was that he was a bit long in the leg and, the shepherd said, 'We don't want to breed no hurdle jumpers.'

Next morning the shepherd said, 'Come and help me to raddle them tups in the nag stable.' He had mixed up raddle, a red powder with oil, in an oil paint tin and made a flat spoon-shaped stick out of a piece of old ash hurdle bar, and he sat the rams up while I handed him the tin and the flat stick and he painted on their flat breasts a covering of half an inch of red paste.

Now to drive four young rams half a mile to the ewes in the far ham would have been difficult so we brought the ewes along to the sheep pens in the yard. There were two hundred of them and by the use of a special gate in the pens we got them into two separate hundreds. Two rams were put with each hundred ewes. One lot we drove up on to the Leasow and the other on to Paris Hill. The rams soon started work on 30 September. 'If we be alive and well we will be lambing late in February,' the shepherd said. Every day or two he caught the rams and raddled them. This went on for three weeks, then he changed the colour to blue, and changed two rams from one flock to the other and vice versa. By working in this way the shepherd knew that the ones marked red would lamb first and could part them at lambing time.

Shakespeare said: 'Put a young ram with an old ewe and you will get good results.' This is what we were doing, a ram lamb and a three-year-old ewe. The shepherd still had some of last year's lambs (tegs) to clear up the sprout stems on Bredon in the winter. He told me once he had hurdled or penned his sheep on every mortal thing on the farm bar the gillies. 'Sprouts, runner beans, peas, cabbage, swedes and sparrowgrass.'

'Asparagus, surely not, Shepherd,' I said.

'Oi, I have, Fred my boy. When Master Carter and yer Dad grew their cabbage plants up between the newly-made beds of sparrowgrass, as usual they didn't want half the plants so I took the ship along and grazed um off.

They be good scavengers, mind ya, but never give um mangels till arter Christmas. Thur's no sugar in um.'

The old Cross Barn, was commonly known as the Sheep Barn, the shepherd having pride of place for its use. Its thatched roof was moss covered; it was timber built with square panels filled with wattle and daub, and had two doors on massive hinges fastened by a hinge asp and staple, beat out on the anvil by the local blacksmith long since laid to rest. These doors were in the middle with another two off-side; each set, when thrown wide open, big enough for the largest of waggons to pass through. The floor was made of blue lias flag stones, level and clean. On the right of the door the sheep pens stood, with the little door to the fold that seems to me so biblical. The partition walls were of elm, sawn long ago in the old Squire's saw pit.

When Shepherd Corbisley was lambing his ewes in the barn, he made little private wards for the mothers, divided by thatched hurdles. A hurricane lamp swung from a broken plough trace was all the light he had.

Old Cross Barn (the sheep barn) and Cross Cottage, where Oliver Hampton lodged with Aunt Phoebe

Here were his headquarters where he fussed the weakly lambs and drenched the ailing ewe.

I was not officially allowed in the lambing pen. We were not supposed to know the facts of life or death at such an early age. But there were ways and means of getting into the old Cross Barn and watching the shepherd act as midwife, doctor, and sometimes as undertaker, sexton and high priest. Sheep, as Job Barley remarked, won't stand the same punishment as a cow. The shepherd never reckoned to take his clothes off during lambing, but Dad took over every day from five o'clock tea-time until ten-thirty at night, when the old shepherd had a nap on the sofa at home.

Later in the year the shepherd did his shearing on a large hessian sheet spread over the threshing floor. His hand shears clipped away all day and shone like silver as they went through the egg-yolk-coloured wool near the sheep. His fleeces were rolled so tightly they could have been kicked all around the barn. These were stacked on a staging made of hurdles so that the air could circulate and prevent mould.

Much of the year, though, the shepherd was with his sheep, up on Bredon Hill, and as a boy I thought that this was the life that I would like most.

THE NEW PLOUGHBOY

Due partly to illness, partly to laziness, I fell very behind with lessons at the Grammar School in Evesham. I pleaded with Dad to let me leave school the Christmas before the School Certificate, and succeeded.

On my last day, the Doc said, 'Archer, what are you going to do?'

'A farmer, sir.'

'Um,' came the retort, 'You will have to farm with your feet. You've no brains.'

School uniform was thrown aside as soon as I had saved enough money to buy clothes which I thought fit for working in the country. The shops closed late on Saturday nights and I was determined to look like an under-carter, shepherd or cowman. The Bedford cord breeches with leather strapping smelt a bit for a time and Mother said the grey tweed jacket, with a poacher's pocket big enough to hold two rabbits, looked like those worn by inmates of the Workhouse. Still, cousin Tom, who had been in the Worcesters, showed me how to put on my puttees to complete the outfit. Plough and Harrow brand boots were waterproof, and had hobnails which made sparks on the road after dark, but they were heavy as lead and gave me blisters until I had softened them with dubbin and neatsfoot oil and broken them in. Dad said, 'It's like breaking in a horse. They call us clodhoppers, but that's about it on the land.'

'I suppose you'd better help Tom Wheatcroft with the cattle,' Dad said. 'He's got a lot to fodder on the hill and the calves to rear.'

Just to be with Tom and help him load the kerves of hay into the muck cart was very satisfying. We fed the out-wintered stores, all heifers, all dark red Herefords, with hay on the frozen hill. Then Tom carried a sack of kibbled cake from Great Hill Barn and put a few pounds into each feeding tub, made of small half-barrels by Oliver. When the snow covered the thatch of the hay rick and he stripped off the icy straw and pulled out the rick pegs for me to stack in a heap under the wall, he would stop for a minute and breathe the warm air from his moustache-capped mouth into his numb fingers. 'Allus the same when I have to start another cut on the rick,' he said. 'Either snowing, freezing or blowing a gale.' When the straw was off, Tom climbed the ladder to cut the hay into square kerves throwing the first burden down for me to stack onto the cart.

The heifers bawled over the gate, waiting for breakfast, dinner and tea all in one. As the knife cut through the hay by the sheer weight and strength of Tom's bent body, the rick stood like a cake on a tea table. Why were the hay cutters so particular about keeping straight? A pride in their work; no other reason. The rick lasted no longer for it.

As I led Turpin with the cart-load of fodder across the flat of Spring Hill, Tom scattered the hay in a straight line as he shuppicked it from the tail of the cart. The heifers followed us and after they hooved each other for the best position, they settled down to feed on the honey-scented cured grass of the previous June. This was the boy I wanted to be. Working with Tom. Listening to his experiences of winters long ago, and wondering how he knew so much of life in general and why he was so content.

Those happy days on the hill were better still when I rode Kitty, the little mare which Dad bought me for a pound a leg at Candlemas Fair.

Some winter days the snow lay in the gullies which the cart had made and everywhere looked the same as the weak rays of the wintry sun shone on the scene. Tom would simply say, 'White world this morning, Fred bwoy.' Nothing could be seen but the footprints of rabbits, hares and foxes — patterns in the snow which told us where they went to earth or form. The twittering of skylarks and the plaintive call of peewits in the spring were a promise of better weather to come. Nature worked very slow but very sure.

In that first spring of working regularly on the land, I was sent as Walt's ploughboy. I thought that I knew everything there was to know about

Ploughing with a four-horse team. The horses, starting from the front, were: the Foremost,
the Body horse, the Lash horse and the Filler

horses, but was soon disillusioned when we went to plough the Thurness with four horses. The ground had been ploughed in the autumn, and we were ploughing it back in March. We started at seven in the morning, chilled by a cold biting wind. Walt said it was a 'skinny wind from Russia'. Our team was Turpin foremost, Boxer and Flower body and lash horse in the middle of the team, and old Captain as filler drawing up the rear. The teams of a hundred years before would have been exactly the same. The fill horse or filler is mentioned in Shakespeare's *The Merchant of Venice*: 'Thou hast got more hair on thy chin than Dobbin my Fill-horse has on his tail.'

It was a hard job. The walking was bad, as we were walking on old furrows. I wore out a ten-shilling pair of boots in the first week. Walt said the ground mooted or muffled, which meant it didn't slip cleanly off the sheel board of the plough, and he had to clean off the clay with the plough paddle kept for this purpose in a little ledge in the throat of the plough.

'Ett,' shouted Walt when Boxer or Turpin left the furrow and walked on the unploughed land. 'Awr,' he called as the horses went too far over on the ploughing. Thurness means 'Thor's nose', and that was the shape of this field, like a giant's nose. On the addledum (headland) the commands were not unlike those of a military manoeuvre. 'Turn come agun' or 'Come agun'

114

Walt said if we were casting a bed of land or turning to the left. 'Turn jinkum' or 'Jig agun' if we were ridging a land or turning right.

The team started to pull unevenly when we came to the 'addledum'. With whip in hand and walking backwards I led Turpin first up to the hedge, turned, 'come agun' and timed it so that each horse did his whack and pulled the plough as far as he could before following Turpin at right angles to the furrow along the headland. If I had kept Turpin's traces tight, the next horse would have followed without going to the end. The first three horses did as they were supposed to, and it was left for Captain, the filler, to pull the plough himself the last few yards. Walt started shouting, 'Awr, come 'ee back,' as Captain ran off into the ploughed ground and the plough ran easy but made a nasty crook in the furrow. I hadn't kept the traces of the middle horses tight enough by shouting 'Come on, Boxer. Yup, Flower,' and cracking the whip. If this happened many times Walt said, 'We'a got a furrow crookeder than a dog's hind leg,' and we had to take some pikes or short turns to right matters. This was done by turning the team and ploughing the last few yards again. Captain was experienced; I was green and if I cracked the whip Turpin would take me through the hedge. He was a powerful gelding and it was not unusual for him to break the traces.

Ploughing never went just right for Walt. He liked to see the clay soil come up shining like rashers of bacon, an unbroken furrow from one end of the ground to the other.

Dad said, 'I reckon Fred ought to go in for a parson as he doesn't care whether the cow calves or the bull breaks his neck.' And this winter I almost decided farming wasn't for me. The work was long and tedious and there always was a great weight of clay sticking to my boots. I was a smallish lad; Walt told me to go and stand in the bull muck and I should shoot up like a poplar tree.

After a time we got a better understanding, Walt, me, Flower, Boxer, Captain and Turpin. Dad and Mr Carter were pleased with the way I was shaping. I learnt a lot from Walt and the determined plodding behind the plough as work went on day in, day out, with the music of jingling harness.

Saturday mornings I usually took one or two horses to the blacksmith's in the village to have them reshod. That was a day out. I rode off full of instructions from Walt. 'Bring me some cart nails, some horse nail stubs and shut links.'

The shut link was linked to the two broken ends of the trace and closed up to form an extra link; the village blacksmith had no welding apparatus but shut two white-hot pieces of iron together to form his weld, hammering them on the anvil until they became one piece.

When we had ploughed back the Thurness twenty-one acres at the rate of three-quarters of an acre a day, Mr Carter and Dad decided that a scuffling both ways with a nine-tined Larkworthy scuffle would kill the squitch (couch grass) and get the ground in good order. Walt and I put four horses, two abreast, on this heavy implement which brought up big 'clats' of clay for the wind and sun to 'lax'. We had Turpin and Boxer on the front, coupled together by a coupling stick. I had to lead them with Walt driving Captain and Old Dick behind.

Now Boxer and Turpin, although they were brothers, were about as much alike as chalk and cheese. Turpin was always raring to go. One word and he lurched forward; a crack of the whip and he would pull me almost under his feet. Boxer was Walt's pet and he knew it; he lagged behind Turpin about a yard and made the foremost pair of our team look untidy. I touched him up a bit with the whip sometimes, but Walt said, 'Don't thee get a waling that hoss. He's a doing his shot.' Old Dick was a biter. He would have gone as a war horse in 1914 but for his big knee. He matched Captain who had a ridged backbone, as I found to my discomfort riding him down the hill from haymaking.

We cleaned the Thurness that Spring, Walt finishing the job by giving it the once-over with the duckfoot drags, a heavy harrow with feet like ducks. He didn't need me for this as he drove three horses abreast.

God said unto Adam, 'In the sweat of thy face shalt thou eat bread,' and a long time ago, when I was a boy, this prediction seemed so true. Men worked in the twenties and thirties as their fathers had done. Seeing men going home at night scuffing their hobnailed boots, tired out with hard labour, was real to me. It was as if there was something extremely virtuous in an aching back and sore feet. The fact was that if someone of my generation had the pluck to suggest an easier way of doing a job, he would be frowned on as a shuffler; someone who was collar proud. 'Collar proud' described a Monday morning work-shy horse who jibbed when the check lining of the collar tightened on his shoulders, shoulders that had been free from work on Sunday.

I can picture Dad returning from the hot July hayfields, his flannelette shirt soaked with sweat, hay seeds in the rim of his straw hat, sitting over supper and Mother saying to him, 'You've overdone it again.'

'More people rust out than wear out,' Dad told us as he experienced the indescribable enjoyment of his well-earned supper, his armchair and evening paper.

7

Changes

THE MOTOR CAR

The real heyday of steam had passed some years before I was born, but as a boy I could still watch the steam waggons fill their tanks with water at the Turn Pike. They dropped their hoses in a ditch where the watercress grew. As they pumped away, a little steam hissed from a pipe by the short funnel, steam which made the farm horses lay back their ears and sometimes run away.

These steam waggons, Sentinels, Fodens, usually pulled a trailer and the wheels were shod with solid rubber tyres. Woolastons of Shirley, I remember, hauled Canadian wheat from Avonmouth to Birmingham. Healings of Tewkesbury had a fine fleet of steam road locos. Their No 8 was particularly fast and many a time during the rail strike, the General Strike of 1926, I was sucked along by the slip-stream of Healings No 8 on my bicycle at twenty miles an hour, as I made my way to my new school, the Grammar School at Evesham. But the age of the petrol engine was already with us in the 1920s.

In my earliest memories of our road between Beckford and Elmley there were two or three cars driven at twenty miles per hour. Cars owned by folk from the village; Mr Cambridge, from The Close, had a chaffeur-driven Sunbeam, Mr Church, the dentist, also had a car.

When I had been at Prep school three or four years, Mr Carter, Dad's partner, bought a Studebaker twenty-horse-power tourer. Pedlar Mason from Paris, on the hill, soon taught him to drive. This meant that Bob, Mr Carter's iron-grey pony, was no longer needed to pull the governess cart to markets and sales. Soon after that Dad made a trip to London with Mr Ernest Roberts of Beckford and bought a Sunbeam sixteen-horse-power tourer. Mr Roberts taught him to drive.

Polly, the chestnut mare, grazed Tun Flun, the cow ground, in front of Mr Carter's house with Bob. I watched with great excitement the change in

A 16 hp Sunbeam Tourer similar to that owned by Tom Archer

pattern as Messrs Archer and Carter drove to market and drove to Cheltenham, shopping. They decided to sell their cobs together. I suppose boys are always eager to see progress. To me the change from one-horse-power to sixteen- and twenty-horse-power seemed a wonderful thing. But how did my elders feel, I wonder? For together they had bought the governess carts new from Birmingham. And what craftsmanship there was in those Rolls-Royces of the end of the horse age! The shafts were made in a particularly tough wood, shafts which would stand the weight of a heavy cart-horse's clumsy hooves. They were sprung like India rubber. The wheels had polished brass hub caps and every spoke fitted into the felly of the wheel as if it grew there. The rubber tyres were noiseless on the roads. 'Turnouts', these family horse carts were called, and Mr Carter and Dad had driven Bob and Polly in turnouts to be proud of.

When I saw Ponto polish Polly's brown harness on the wall of our courtyard, no thoughts of regret entered my mind over the Studebaker and Sunbeam takeover. No doubt Ponto polished Bob's harness for Mr Carter. It was black and shining to blend with the iron grey of Bob.

The day came when the mare and gelding friends of Tun Flun went to what was known as the Repository at Cheltenham to be sold. Dad sold the complete turnout. Mr Bailey retained the governess cart – perhaps he thought he might need it again one day. Min and Tom, the two nags which pulled the market drays and milk float, remained in Tun Flun for me.

In Mr Carter's motor house under the dovecote stood the coach-built car with its brass lamps – just one more of the kings which were fast taking over our roads. Cart-horses from our stable were moved to the nag stable where Bob and Polly once stood and one Saturday morning Oliver Hampton brought his frail basket of tools to convert our stable into a motor house, they weren't called garages then, for LX 4415. He widened the doors and made a drive, put up two gate posts and spent a whole day placing a flat stone between the gate posts. With a brace and an old bit, he bored a hole in the stone for the gate fastener to drop into. This focal point had to be measured over and over again until the exact spot was found for the double gates to be fastened securely. The Sunbeam came over from Grafton where Mr Roberts had housed it and there it stood alongside the stable manger.

How well I remember Dad driving the Sunbeam through the yard and into the motor house the first time, and a trial run up Stanway Hill with Tom and me sheltering on the back seat behind the middle screen of glass under a leather apron. And was it cold at Stow-on-the-Wold!

Wellington boots in the early twenties were rare. I never saw a landworker wearing them. But when Dad went to London he not only bought the car, he also bought a pair of Wellingtons and what he called a 'hoose-pipe' for cleaning them. Another novelty for me. Hoses on taps I'd never seen before.

Cleaning the car was a ritual. The wooden wheel spokes were brushed and the hose-pipe swilled off most of the dirt and dust. Brasso for the lamps. Brasso for the hub caps. And the hose-pipe proved useful in quite a different way. When the weather was dry the wooden spokes became loose from the hub to the wheel rim. Water from the hose soon tightened them up again and this became a regular treatment in hot, dry weather.

Loose spokes were always referred to as 'talking'. In a waggon, for instance, when the wheels creaked and groaned under the load of hay the carter would say, 'Don't them spokes talk. We shall have to soak the wheels in the horse pond.'

Our car, was grey with black wings, complete with klaxon horn, a spare tin of Pratt's petrol locked onto the rubber-covered running board, and was never cleaned with any sophisticated polish. Water on the body and Cherry Blossom boot polish on the wings, or mudguards.

At thirty miles per hour maximum the back axle seemed to sing a tune. 'Warmed up now,' Dad said.

THE TELEPHONE

Before the telephone came to Ashton in the early 1920s, messages and news were sent and received by telegram. There were the everyday wires for farmers like Dad and Mr Dunn which might read 'Expect cattle at Beckford Station on the five-twenty' from a Shropshire vendor. There were also those which carried more momentous news.

'My poor old aunt at Nottingham has passed away,' Kate Dunn told Millie and was overheard by Jimmy Blizzard who remarked,

'Thur's a funny thing, passed away, my relatives allus died. Some be called and some falls asleep according to the stones in the churchyard, but mine have allus died most on um natural like.'

Then Tat Lippet had a wire, 'Please meet me off the seven o'clock, I'm coming for a week. Loving sister Elsie.' 'That's the missus's sister from Brum,' said he. 'Shan't get a word in edgeways now. They allus comes when my plums be ripe, thur's no doubt the guardsvan ull be loaded with plums and runner byuns. Still her allus brings us a bit of ham from the market hall.'

Down at the station along the branch line from Evesham to Ashchurch stood telegraph poles with wires in between. Wires which sang in the wind, buzzed and oscillated. In the room marked 'Booking Office, Private', the Morse code was tapped out on the board. The porter-in-charge and the under-porter took no notice of these pips and squeaks until they recognised their own particular code calling Ashton Station. Then and only then they listened for the telegrams which came every day. These messages in Morse from faraway places were written down on forms printed for the purpose. The forms were folded in little buff envelopes and despatched to their destination by the under-porter, full speed on his bike.

It is interesting that there was opposition to the telephone, not from the native-born villagers but from the settlers from Birmingham, who looked for beauty and art and decided that telephone wires and poles had neither. Ten subscribers eventually had the phone installed.

The Post Office then replaced the blacksmith's as the centre of the village grapevine. Here people found out about the latest market prices, a scandal or two, and discovered why the trains were running late. The manually-operated exchange with only ten subscribers had its advantages. The postmaster could tell us that the party we were calling was not at home but in The Star. But he was discreet, and though he must have heard many village secrets, he never gossiped.

The Post Office at Ashton-under-Hill

THE WIRELESS

This underdeveloped village and its people, apart from the few retired city gentlemen, had never heard music apart from village concerts. The Church held an affair known as the Armistice Tea where men who had fought in the Great War sang songs from the trenches. Ladies who had been to festivals at Cheltenham sang with men of the choir pieces by Gilbert and Sullivan. Millie Bostock sang to her own accompaniment *Come into the Garden Maud*. Children's voices, singing happily to Mrs Church's piano, could be heard from the school. The scope was so limited. Gramophones with great horns scratched records by Caruso.

'What are the wild waves saying?' was the slogan at the very beginning of music on tap. I thought of wireless waves as the tide coming into our village seventy miles from the sea, with white horses hitting the rocks. In a way the tide did come in that day when Percy Wigley made his first wireless set and Ray Priday, the under-porter, with cat's whisker and crystal linked us with London for the very first time. I well remember going with my brother to Ray Priday's cottage and together holding the headphones and hearing Big Ben strike six o'clock.

One winter's day Sam Green, an Evesham gramophone shopkeeper, gave a wireless concert in 'The Room'. It was a Saturday and it took all day with a forty-round ladder fixing aerials up to the end of our barn across the rickyard to the Recreation Room. Then great brown insulators were put in position. The local gravedigger volunteered to dig a sizeable hole just outside the doorway. When this was done Sam Green buried an old galvanised iron bath and soldered an earth wire to this. By nightfall the three-valve wireless set with its half-hundredweight accumulator and another dry battery was oscillating. Howard Cambridge said he knew it was going to be a wireless concert for he had been down to 'The Room' and seen the wires.

'It's nothing but works of the Devil,' said one man the other side of Bredon Hill.

'No doubt it ull upset the weather,' was Uncle George's prediction. That was what he used to say about changing the clocks. He used to talk of 'God's time'. Country folk who had sung around the piano and held concerts in the Room were suspicious of the wireless.

Ernest Roberts, a dab hand at anything mechanical, started making three-valve sets for the folk who could afford twenty pounds. It took all day to install one. The high aerial, the insulators and the sunken bucket for the earth wire were all a part of the early wireless outfits. A low-tension battery, weighing fifty-six pounds and a high-tension one, then the coils which were changed for different stations. 2 LO seemed to be our station when our set arrived.

I can still see the horn loudspeaker on the dresser, the set on a small table and the big battery on the floor. Dad turned the knob which moved the coils closer together or farther apart. Squeals came from the horn speaker, then oscillations up and down the scale. A bit of practice, then Peter Eckersley's voice was loud and clear. 'This is 2 LO calling, 2 LO. . . .' on so many metres. Then we sat around and listened to John Henry and Blossom, a comedy act. ·We were in touch with London and Birmingham. Shepherd Corbisley and his wife came with Uncle George some evenings.

'Well I'm dalled,' the shepherd said as he looked out at the starry night. 'A hundred miles to London and I've yeard Big Ben.' The shepherd looked up at the night sky and still wondered, as we all did, how this marvel had been born.

I still went some Sunday nights to listen and join in when I could to the singing around Aunty Lucy's cottage organ. Cousin Mary played and pedalled away at the carpeted pedals. But the news, saxophones, whether one liked it or not, jazzed throughout the village.

MORE CHANGES

At the age of five, I had been fascinated by the flush WC at Prep school. Now we were to be one of the few households in the village with a WC and a proper bath. My mother's brother was a builder, and came over in a slack period to convert a bedroom into a bathroom. He installed a bath and a boiler, and a WC with a sewer pipe to the septic tank which was positioned next to the outdoor privy. We loved pulling the chain, but Dad told us to keep the WC only for emergencies and to go on using the garden privy.

There was a golden glow on a winter's night as the oil lamps hung from the beams above the white damask tablecloths as the villagers had tea. Points of flame from the uneven lamp wicks were a constant worry. Globes or glass funnels from the grocer cost about eightpence and a store of these, wrapped in newspaper, lay in the dresser or chest of drawers in most homes. If the hot globe was not upright on the lamp, it touched the cold side of the funnelled shade above and cracked. By candlelight another globe was fixed, by candlelight the uneven wick was trimmed or levelled up by the point of a pocket knife.

Ashton didn't go on to the electric mains until 1934, but well before that,

Dad bought an Aladdin for the new living room which had been made out of the old coal store. Its mantle flame gave a white light, as white as electric light, and shone on the new parquet floor, the grand piano which Dad had bought at a sale and the new three-piece suite. I felt that I preferred the House Place.

8

Church and Chapel

Sundays were a vital part of village life. It was a necessary day of rest for the poor who struggled six days a week, sometimes ten hours a day, to scrape a living from the land. The village was quiet. At home we had breakfast together, even our toys were resting in the wooden cupboard by the piano. After a Sunday dinner which told the season of the year by its vegetables and fruit puddings, the whole village turned out, if it was fine, to walk around, looking at the crops, picking wild flowers, and watching the antics of the cart-horses who seemed to know that it was their rest day too. The women wore flowery hats and dresses made on their sewing-machines, the men their Church or Chapel-going dark suits.

On Sunday evenings in winter we would feel snug from the cold, joining Mother as she sang hymns at the piano. She had a beautiful voice, and used to tell us about the time her music teacher had tried to persuade Grandma to let her become a professional singer.

Apart from Sunday School, I loved those village Sundays.

Boys like me in the 1920s, living in the country, were in the happy position of never even questioning the existence of God. We read in Genesis, Chapter One, that at the close of the sixth day, God saw everything that he had made and behold it was very good. How literally this mystery was acceptable to us varied as we grew and our character developed. The important thing that we inherited from the old and staid villager was that behind everything which went on in the countryside around us was a master hand – some people called it Providence. We believed when the November-planted wheat took perhaps six weeks to come up and the late April-planted barley shot through the warm earth in forty-eight hours that nature was not just an accident but the plan repeated itself from one Christmas Day to another.

'Break Thou the bread of life dear Lord for me.' So sang the Chapel congregation to the harmonium as the group sipped the unfermented wine from egg-cup-like glasses once a month. For the folk of the Established Church, it was a sixteenth-century chalice passed round, brimful with

Sacramento. A nineteenth-century vicar used to say that, 'If God ever laughs, and I'm sure he does, it's when he sees his children refusing to meet at his table.' No one seemed to think it odd that the folk living at the top end of the village walked to the Church at the bottom for the bread and wine, while many from the bottom walked to the Chapel at the top for the same reason.

When I was a boy, the Established Church of St Barbara was Low Church and had excellent relations with the Chapel. This was not always so. Uncle Jim told me of the Revd Gough tolerating the Non-Conformists but describing their open air meetings as entertainments. These meetings, often wrongly timed and badly sited, reinforced by the Salvation Army band, frequently led to trouble in the village.

Toleration was completely lacking. There were faults on both sides. Statements were made at some open-air meetings, intentionally or not, which added fuel to the flames and upset the Anglicans. One of the Squire's keepers threw half a brick through the Mission Hall window, striking an old lady on the head. Since 1912, however, the relations between Church and Chapel in our village have been cordial. Millie Bostock, a very strong

Ashton's old Baptist Chapel where the author was warned against 'Dynamic Debauchery'!

Anglican, gave recitals on the Free Church organ to raise money, the Chapel people attended the special efforts for the Anglican Church.

THE CHAPEL

The Chapel elders might have come from the Outer Hebrides the way they observed Sunday. The solemn, undertaker-like faces, the dark clothes, showed the world as they walked the half-mile village street carrying black Bibles and hymn books that it was Sunday, The Lord's Day. These men frowned even at the occasional child passing on a bike. They considered listening to the wireless on Sunday as a road to perdition. For them it was more of a day of mourning than a day of rest.

Joe Baker and the other elders who ran the Chapel, climbed up the bethel steps in navy suits and flat, pancake caps of grey, or black if a recent death had struck the family. The farmers wore tweeds, broad-banded, silver-grey trilbies. Percy, who took the collection, was what one might call a relic of pre-enclosure days, working four days on the farm and two on his holding where he grew strawberries, onions and plums. Percy walked the carpeted aisle in Bedford cord breeches, leathered inside the knees, pigskin buttoned gaiters and brown polished boots. A smart Harris tweed coat completed his Sunday outfit. Head bowed in front of the rostrum, he looked like a good class bailiff on his way to market as he handed the plate to the preacher.

We sang the hymns of Moody and Sankey to the accompaniment of an orchestra of brass viol, cello, two violins, and sometimes a piano accordion, all played by Joe Baker and his sons and daughters.

'Again,' shouted Joe, if he liked the chorus of the morning hymn, and the music makers gave the refrain as Joe muttered 'Praise The Lord, Hallelujah.'

Joe told us at morning Sunday School of the inescapable sin we had inherited from Adam and of the remedy of the Cross.

'What did the Possle Paul say? . . .' then a quote.

'What did the poet say? . . .' a quote from a well-known hymn.

We were warned of the bottomless pit, the fire and the brimstone of hell, promised a land in eternity where there is no night, nor sorrow, nor crying – a Utopia beyond description for the faithful. Joe declared the wine at the wedding feast at Cana was unfermented like blackcurrant tea. Whist and dancing were works of the devil.

'Them as smokes down yer ull smoke in Hell,' he said, 'and if we was meant to smoke thur ud be a chimney on top of our heads.'

'A Sabbath well spent brings a week of content,' they told us.

On some Sunday nights the preacher came from away. Edward Roberts from Evesham was a Welshman, a dwarf for a blacksmith. He was so short that unless the top part of the pulpit was dismantled when he preached we could only see the top of Edward's head. Sitting in the second seat from the front I didn't miss much.

Edward, after mopping his brow of perspiration (he'd had a hard ride from Evesham), began with these words, 'Let us commence our service with prayer.' One example of Edward's Hywel was when he half sang and half said, 'Jeremiah – was called – the Doleful Prophet – because he wrote the book of Lamentations.' I remember him speaking of the folly of a hurried meal. 'Some people say that every time we speak we miss a mouthful but I think mealtimes should be times of conversation.' Edward was one who prayed for 'our friends at St Barbara's and all worshipping in like manner in spirit and in truth'. A farmer from Beckford took for his subject, 'We are the brothers.' Tom Adams on the Monday went to see him and said, 'You remember what you said about all us being brothers last night?'

The farmer replied, 'Yes, Tom, I do.'

'Could you lend me forty pounds then?'

Charlie Bradfield said, 'Oi, but he wasn't brother enough for that.'

One visiting preacher who shouted, laughed and cried, and rampaged up and down the platform, kicked the collection basket for six up the aisle, just missing me. He shouted, 'Filthy lucre!' and George Foster replied, 'Hallelujah!' He was one of the few old-timers who practised 'button-holing'. This was done by the preacher quietly leaving the stage during the singing of the benediction hymn and being in position in the porch to ask any likely-looking sinner, 'Are you on the Lord's side?' I think it did more harm than good as it kept people away.

I do remember the unorthodox, the mistakes men made, but as a boy with an enquiring mind that was just me.

In between the dour, the amusing, we had a few excellent speakers. There was a devout man from Pershore, Reuben Broad. We knew what his subject would be – Shadrach, Meshach and Abednego in the burning fiery furnace. He was a tall dark-skinned man with closely cropped hair and a heart as good as gold. I could tell you of lots of people he helped through difficult times. He referred to us as 'Ma friends'. Once he forgot to take his cycle clips off his trousers and as he paced the platform did this without interrupting his address. Another hot summer Sunday he came without waistcoat and, with his thumbs linked under his elastic braces, drew the braces forward one at a time to be released like a catapult against his chest. His prayer was a gem, always the same. (Who said we have no ritual?) He started off, 'Lord, remember all who worship Thee, tonight, not only in the cathedrals, the temples, the tabernacles and fine churches throughout the length and breadth of our land, but in the chapels, little bethels and under the canopy of the glorious Heavens; in fact, in every small corner of Thy great vineyard.'

Tom and Bill Windsor, father and son, were both good honest men. Tom rode an ancient tricycle and Bill had a motor-cycle. 'Capital, capital!' was Tom's favourite expression. Bill used words I didn't understand, like 'Dynamic debauchery', but I do remember his usual text, 'Our light affliction, which is just for a moment, is nothing compared with the glory which is to come.' He brought with him the Bidford Nightingale, a counter tenor, to sing falsetto solos which I tried to copy after my voice broke.

There was a cosiness difficult to explain in that little Welsh-type bethel with its black stove, chain-hung brass oil lamps, pitchpine pews, little harmonium a key out of tune, and the platform with a chair and table for the preacher. The heavily perfumed congregation incensed the room as the temperature rose on those Sunday nights. But the perfume varied according to the season and according to the age, state of health of the worshipper.

Joe Meadows smelt of eucalyptus. He took some on sugar all the winter to ward off the 'flu. When he tore his red spotted handkerchief from his pocket the aroma spread like an eastern plantation around the room. The old folk sat at the back near the stove where the camphor, wintergreen, camphorated oil mingled in a heavy cloud overpowering all other scents. Was it true I wonder, that some of the ladies sucked extra strong mints to camouflage the reek of Guiness?

Beyond everything else this cell of Fundamental Christianity thought themselves right with this world and the next. A comfortable thought in days of poverty, that the best is yet to be, although the address (Chapel folk of the laity don't profess to preach sermons) was often twenty minutes of warning that whoever went through the door unsaved might never have another chance to repent, in danger of a Christless grave, a lost eternity.

The Amens, the Hallelujahs, the Praise the Lords died down. *Lord keep us safe this night, secure from all our fears* was played. What fears? The preacher often put the fear of the devil into us enough to ruin the night's rest of all but the Chosen few.

At the Chapel Christmas treat the tea drinkers packed the Recreation Room, and after Christmas puddings with threepenny bits in and the usual brew out of the urns, games began, all the usual: *Sir Roger, A-hunting we will go*, *Clap and run* and *Spinning the trencher*. As the party warmed up Mr Carter came through the door with the strongest waggon rope he could find and a tug-of-war took place in the room until more often than not the winners landed on the stage or down the steps, or the rope broke. We stayed until about ten o'clock when some of the broader-minded Chapel members suggested, 'Let's have a jig round,' and, would you believe it, dancing commenced. Mr Carter didn't object and he paid for the tea so, like David of old, they danced.

THE VILLAGE CHURCH

The whole of the Church of St Barbara spoke of the Bostock family. Tablets of stone in the walls were inscribed with the names of past generations of Bostocks, underfoot the floor was covered with the family's memorials and there was a Bostock vault under the tower.

Millie Bostock played the organ on Sunday nights, and her rendering of *The Funeral March* had to be heard to be believed, for every timber, every pane of glass, clear or stained, resonated when she pulled out the stops and thundered the bass notes.

Revd Vernon lived in the vicarage at Beckford, and rode his tricycle

The interior of the Church of St Barbara

conscientiously between his two parishes. He was a great believer in cocoa, and would take a tin for the sick people he visited, asking them to open the tin before he left so that he could have the coupons which he collected. He was known as a desperate man for a 'bun struggle', and enjoyed the fabulous high teas which Millie Bostock organised for the Mothers' Union. Once he started on the ham before Millie had time to ask him to say grace. The Mothers' Union was not short of women with a sense of humour, and knowing the parson's weakness for doughnuts, they loaded a plate with them and put it in front of him. He usually cleared up the whole plate, and might still have room for the delicious home-made cakes the women rivalled each other in making.

Charlie, the Parish Clerk and sexton, was always called Stocky, being a short man. He read the psalms from the bottom tier of the pulpit, over which was a sound board. For eighty-nine years Stocky lived in his thatched black and white, wattle and daub cottage. Besides making ladders, he made hurdles and gates. He was born in 1858 and he could remember when the village orchestra accompanied the psalms and hymns before the organ was installed.

Stocky was steeped in the ways of High Church under Revd Vernon's predecessor, Revd Gough. His rendering of 'Armen' with a gutteral Gloucestershire accent reverberated under the arched roof. Sometimes he put an extra answer into Revd Gough's intonations. Never was a worshipper able to forget that Stocky was Clerk. His game leg restricted him a little, but the short ash plant, a knobbed walking stick, helped him around the building – it was also useful to whack any mischievous choirboy in the vestry.

Stocky's inimitable way of dousing candles was noticeable to visitors, but accepted as part of the ritual by the villagers. He blew them out one by one with noisy puffs, like an engine letting off steam on threshing days. The doctor, a churchwarden, told him to restrain himself, but to no avail.

When Revd Vernon took over the living, Stocky didn't approve of him. He didn't like his habit of shaking hands with his parishioners as they left the Church, and described him as 'Low Chapel'. Revd Vernon had no success in restraining Stocky with his loud 'Armens'.

Parson Vernon excelled at funerals. He had a voice full of comfort to rich and poor alike. It was Stocky who tolled the bell announcing a funeral in the village. He limped in front of the funeral procession, next to the vicar, as the bier borrowed from the next village creaked its way down the rough village street, the bearers wearing black-turned-green suits and shallow ancient bowler hats.

Stocky was still gravedigger in our churchyard when I was a boy. 'How's thee father?' he asked my friend as we watched him throw the blue clay subsoil out of the grave bottom ready to take an old soldier who had fought in the Zulu War.

'Better, Stocky,' said my friend.

'And he had better be or else I'll have him in yur,' said Stocky.

I doubt if Stocky meant to be callous but he had grown up to his job and so had his father before him. We talked to him about the old soldier about to be buried as he sat on a gravestone and drank cider out of a horn cup and ate his bread and cheese and fat bacon.

The churchyard lay alongside the moat and the park field where we played in the holidays. It was my eighth birthday and one of my aunts had bought me a football. We played until the funeral. As we leant over the churchyard wall, we saw Soldier Jim carried shoulder high, his coffin covered in the Union Jack, and heard the bugle blow the Last Post. We were very quiet and after the lowering into the grave, Stocky's next office, when the parson said, 'Ashes to ashes, dust to dust,' was to sprinkle some fine earth on the coffin. Stocky was not unkind, but uncouth, unlearned, and whack, whack, whack, the box resounded as he dropped great clods of blue clay on to the coffin. The vicar mentioned this to him, but Stocky was unconcerned, saying, 'Old Jim and me a bin pals all our life and he udn't a wanted nothing different. He udn't a wanted me a gone to the trouble to riddle a bit a fine stuff just to go on top of him. Old Jim's all right under that yew tree, I be gwain to lie anant him one day.'

This was my first experience of a funeral. After Stocky had filled in the grave, we crept up to the lonely flowers, and I wondered, thinking that the man sleeping under the yews was nearly eighty years older than me, and we started the football again until tea-time. Tea in a tent made from a rick sheet by Dad, among the apple blossom in Lammas hay orchard. Jelly and blancmange.

Within the compound of our village, gossip was rife, and any bit of spicy news oiled the wheels of life, but nevertheless it seemed as if no one was beyond the pale in Ashton, although Millie Bostock and the Chapel elders might fear for the sinners' salvation.

Church and Chapel both had large congregations then, and, as old Tom Wheatcroft told me, 'The Chapel a-gin you a good staddle (foundation) and you a-got to pick the meat off the bones.'

The old shepherd was very close to the soil and to all living things except his fellow men. He only mixed at busy times; otherwise his life was lonely.

He started mowing early, often at first light; and when the mid-day sun was pouring down, the horses were rested in the shade . . .

9

Village Politics

THE WAR MEMORIAL

Our village, numbering three hundred or so, was united in times of hardship, especially during the poverty of the late nineteenth century and the 1914–18 war. But those of us who have experienced the ups and downs of village life in times of peace and comparative plenty, know that divisions just come from nowhere. Two cricket teams had played their matches quite independently for years just because of a personal quarrel between two farmers when Ashton Cricket Club was first set up. Such is the independence of the men of the land. 'Stomachful' Tom Wheatcroft called it, but there has always been that extra bit of stubbornness under the belt of these men.

Village politics were every bit as intense over more fundamental matters. After the bonfire and fireworks celebrating the end of the war, folk began talking about erecting a permanent memorial to serve as a reminder of those we had lost, ten good men out of forty-eight who served in the forces. Several were badly wounded, and those who had suffered most were the most loath to talk about it. The meeting held in the school to discuss a site for the War Memorial was, to say the least, tempestuous. This was unfortunate and there were faults on both sides. The new owner of the Croft, Mr Cambridge had a spinney on the boundary of his property. This had been enclosed many years ago by the previous owner – a financier named Saunderson – and added to the Croft. Mr Cambridge, known by everyone as 'the Old Gentleman', from the kindness of his heart offered the village this small spinney opposite the school as a site for the memorial.

'It yunt his to give,' said Gunner Wood who was still smarting from his wounds, the effects of poison gas and two years in a German prison camp. 'That land belongs to the village. It's the old pound and our old chap can mind the time when stray cattle and sheep were impounded there, afore old Saunderson pinched it. Yunt that right, Ernest?' he said to Ernest Bradfield who was sitting by him.

'It's the sartin truth,' Ernest agreed.

This really started the trouble about the memorial site. The natives resented the fact that the Old Gentleman was giving away something that really belonged to the village. After much discussion the doctor in the chair said the answer was a ballot and a date was chosen to hold this in the school. By an overwhelming majority the supporters of the Pound won the election.

'We won't be done,' said Joe Baker, who had lost a son in France. Ernest Bradfield had, as Tom said 'bin further afield' – Salonika, and that was where he said the war was won.

Ernest was a fine figure of a man who wore a black bowler on Armistice Days, marching slightly ahead, shoulders forward and body upright which gave a waltzing effect as he followed the ex-servicemen and the Tewkesbury band playing *Colonel Bogey*. The row of medals across his broad chest were about the maximum that the lapel of his coat would carry and they swayed and jingled like a martingale on some great horse pulling a brewer's dray.

For weeks after the meeting, the money had been pouring in to pay for the Portland stone cross to be erected in the Pound. The Opposition had held their meetings at the full moon with Pedlar Mason as their leader. Pedlar was a small market-gardener and fruit grower, and a highly-respected employer, of the hamlet of Paris. He liked to stir things up. His only son had been gassed on the Western Front and had developed TB, and Pedlar was understandably bitter. He had no time for King and Country. To say Pedlar was a Socialist would be putting it mildly. He was left of left, working towards the revolution as had been recently witnessed in Russia. He came from Coventry where he learnt the motor trade, dabbled in gardening in the city parks and took up taxi work in his spare time. He was a great reader of Marxist philosophy, a student of Darwin, an admirer of Trotsky, and of course anti-Church. In fact, he was anti everything the villagers had held dear for centuries. But they admired him as a constant defender of the poor and the unfortunate, competing with the vicar in their relief. A sandy-haired little man with a broad grin, smoking an everlasting Woodbine, he drove a Model T Ford.

Sapper Allen was also one of the anti-Pound lot. He lived in one of those outlying cottages, built on no-man's-land, an old roadside verge or corner. Not so much stolen, as reclaimed after the enclosures of common land at the end of the eighteenth century. Sapper, a plasterer without equal, raised ten children in his house, which he had turned into a miniature sham castle. Two stone balls cast by him sat on squared pillars at the entrance to his small barn where he practised his art with the most primitive of tools. Templates and moulds hung on the walls, and there were potters' wheels on the bench for plaster work. Pseudo-Norman arches led up to the damson orchard, ornate flower pots on stems encircled with plaster serpents spilled red geraniums. Sapper started his week Tuesday after Monday recovering from a weekend on Ashton cider. His art was in great demand, restoring churches, cathedrals and Georgian houses, and he did much work on Tewkesbury Abbey.

Pedlar was continually making cracks at the Old Gentleman, the doctor, George Hughes the artist, Ernest Roberts a retired engineer, and all the upper crust of our village who supported the Pound site. He composed verses and stuck his efforts on Stocky Hill's front door, which was never opened, and on the two elm trees in the hedgerow of our rickyard. The raising of the money and the planning of the memorial all took time and Pedlar was trying to put a question mark in people's minds. 'He'll end up in clink (Gloucester Jail) as sure as hell's a mousetrap,' said the quiet, deep thinking Shepherd Corbisley, but Pedlar knew just how far to go.

With very little help Sapper Allen started a rival memorial in his yard just in front of his barn. This Memorial was a masterpiece, it just grew from a square base – first one step and then the next, all done in cement and granite chippings, trowelled and dowelled, skimmed and floated. The *pièce de résistance* was a laurel wreath which would round the upright pillar, like a boa constrictor. The top was finished by a cross and he covered it with a Union Jack.

Speculation grew to fever pitch as the money had almost been raised to erect the official memorial in the Pound, and a Cheltenham builder had been commissioned to make it. It was Whitsuntide and the weather was ideal for the early haymaking and, most important, for our annual Whit Monday cricket match against Alcester and Ragley Park. This was an all-day match; the Old Gentleman gave a salad lunch to all who wished to attend and, needless to say, most of the villagers were there. I stayed for lunch but came home for tea so that I could help Tom Wheatcroft, our cowman, suckle the calves and tell him the score.

'Frederick, I s'pose thee hast noticed what's a gwain on on the village green by the Cross?' he said.

'No, Tom, I came the yard way,' I said.

'Well, thee pop across the rickyard and have a look. Dalled if I knows what thee father and them gentlemen down at the match ull say when stumps be drawn.' I went and looked between the two giant elms. The hawthorn was gone out of blow and the elder, or ellun, gave out that intoxicating scent. There, in the middle of the green, was a group of enthusiastic, sincere men, stripped to their striped Oxford shirts, making the concrete foundation for Sapper's memorial. Not if I live to be a hundred shall I ever see again such an act of sheer audacity being done with such precise timing. A square of well made concrete, mixed by Ernest, Joe, Pedlar Mason and Gunner Wood, was being levelled by Sapper Allen with his plasterer's trowel and spirit level. It set as hard as 'the devil's backside' said Old Stodge, our roadman.

The Council stepped in the next day and gave an order that no more building was to be done on the green. Stodge was ordered to break the concrete, but Sapper had put something in the mixture which defied Stodge's pickaxe and it remained covered with soil and grass for many years until the signpost was erected. During hot dry summers the square brown patch still showed in the midst of our village green, and Sunday dinner-times when Sapper was primed to the full and smoking his cherry pipe which held almost half an ounce of twist tobacco, he would click his heels together, remove his cap and give a solemn salute where his memorial might have been. Then as he wended his way around the many corners of

The Ashton-under-Hill War Memorial, unveiled on 8 November 1924

Gipsies Lane he sang *Tipperary* and shouted to us boys in a kind of pidgin French.

As for the official Memorial, on 8 November 1924 the Cornish Cross, with a sword pointing downwards, upon a pedestal and steps, was unveiled by General Sir Francis Davies of Elmley Castle.

My father was among several villagers who welcomed the General. The inscription was on one side with the names of the fallen carved underneath. On the other side we read these words which I think explain everything that happened in those grim years: 'These were a wall unto us, both by night and day.' It was sad that the little group who favoured Sapper's memorial refused to have their relations' names put on this memorial; but later they relented.

THE PARISH COUNCIL

Dr Overthrow had been our Councillor for much longer than I could remember. Being a little man, he always sat on the minute book to give him a bit more height. He had served the village well on Parish Council, Rural District Council and every other council, except the County Council. This gave him a status in village life. It's true that the old and poor amongst his patients were reminded to vote for him when he did his rounds, and were told that he had never sent them a bill, and neither would he if they voted for him.

He was a nominal Tory, with connections in the Cheltenham constituency, and ran the Ashton Club, a branch of the Cirencester and Tewkesbury Conservative Sick and Dividend Society. But he lost his zest for the Tory cause in later life, partly through his feud with the Tory Bostock family, and also because of his sympathies with the aged and infirm labouring folk, who were not generously treated under the Poor Law, with a Bostock as Guardian.

One of his last fights on the Council was against the proposal to pipe the stream which followed the roadside in front of Rockland House. It was a pretty stream, crossed by little stone-built causeways or bridges to the gateways of the cottages. Some said he was against the scheme because his little flock of Khaki Campbell ducks swam in the stream and sometimes laid their eggs in the sparkling spring water. He lost his fight and Ashton lost its stream.

Pedlar Mason hated the Bostocks, and the Cambridge family who had bought Bostock property and who owned and farmed half the land in the village. He too wanted to better the lot of the working man. The closest that Pedlar could get to his socialist ideas was to form a local branch of the Labour Party. Jasper the coalman lived opposite the Star Inn, and was always eager to earn a shilling. He put his front room at their disposal for a rent of half-a-crown (30p). It was here in this bare room with cardboard replacing a broken window and age-old white geraniums on the sill, that the Party was formed.

Jasper was joined by the farm labourers, Ern and Harry, and Sapper the plasterer, ex-servicemen from the 1914 war, and the blacksmith. Pedlar's son Darwin had been to Ruskin College, Oxford, and gave lectures in Jasper's cottage on Marxist doctrine.

The doctor formed a kind of alliance with Pedlar because he wanted Pedlar and Harry on the Parish Council to help him oppose the Bostocks and their friends.

Mr Cambridge, the big landowner, was incensed by Pedlar, who incited the men to refuse to work overtime without an allowance of cider, boiled bacon and bread, and encouraged them to poach rabbits from the Hill as their right. Mr Cambridge, whose green-liveried chauffeur drove him to his first-class carriage for Birmingham, was furious that a man with only two acres and an orchard could afford to run a car, and was jealous of the bumper crops of cherries and strawberries that Pedlar grew in Paris, above the frost line.

When the doctor became too deaf to hear the motions proposed and seconded, it was time for him to retire from the Parish Council, and an election was arranged. Pedlar persuaded four of his friends to stand with him against the staid Big Five of the Establishment. Despite the canvassing at the pub and over the billiard table at the Recreation Room, none of Pedlar's party was elected. But the village never forgot that dusty day in May when Pedlar and Harry drove furiously to collect the old and infirm for the polling booth.

Pedlar was a man before his time, for change comes slowly to a village. The old order, feudal in a way, was a prop for the villagers to lean on. It's true that some lived in tied cottages, homes that went with their jobs, but they were not a lot of yes-men. Rather, they were dubious of Pedlar's extreme thinking, trusting more in the status quo policy of James Cambridge and his other four councillors.

After the parish election, Pedlar from Paris and his friends were not satisfied with the result; they said it was a kind of frame up. One Sunday morning, after Dad had been nominated for the Rural District Council, the village was plastered with printed posters. I remember one which said,

'Beware of the wolf in sheep's clothing. They have had you over the Parish Council, don't let them have you over the District Council.' Folk going to Church and Chapel that Sunday were flabbergasted at a verse about one of Ashton's leaders. The name he was given, Bummy Cambridge, had never been associated with him before, and the printer omitted to print his own name at the foot of the poster. That week, as the messages of dissatisfaction were pinned on elm trees, make-shift notice boards and Stocky's front door, the whole place buzzed with speculation.

Solicitor's opinion was that the parish pump politicians had just kept within the law. The printer was in error but no action was taken.

And so, with a stormy beginning, Dad succeeded Dr Overthrow as village member on the RDC and member of the Guardians Committee.

Even then there was a need for council houses for the village and soon a plot was found on the Elmley Road, and a local builder built our first eight houses. The rent for these, including rates, was about four shillings a week. And so the village grew with me.

I thought then how grand the houses were compared with the thatched hovels the landworkers had lived in. Black and white and thatch cottages, however pretty on postcards, are grim inside before modernisation. Condemned as unfit for human habitation, they stood as empty sepulchres for more years than I care to think.

AN EXTRAORDINARY PARISH MEETING

The first big decision Dad had to make came a little later on the Council agenda. More houses had been built, still at a rent that the farm worker and his wife could pay by thrift and good management. A few of these houses, however, were allocated to families a notch higher in the social scale, better off than the thirty-shillings-a-week men on the land. I heard of men getting two pounds ten shillings a week in Evesham.

These people were not content to carry drinking water from the standpipe taps of the village street. It had been such a familiar sight, something I had thought inevitable.

A couple of new private houses went up and were connected to the council main. The two-pound-ten-a-week men wanted to be connected to the village water supply, but the pressure in the pipes was too low and the RDC could do nothing, as the council houses stood at the highest point in the village.

All the water came from Paris on the Hill, from three reservoirs. The council main was a second-hand Cheltenham gas-pipe, sixty years old. This provided water for the houses on that estate, and for our farm, Mr Carter's farm and the Cross cottages. There were various wells still being used, but Paris was the place oozing with water, enough to supply several villages, but not high enough up the hill to push it to the council houses themselves.

I was always interested in the Parish Meetings, and I attended the Annual Parish Meeting at an early age. Not being a ratepayer and not having a vote, I just sat and listened.

The question of the water supply caused quite a stir. An Extraordinary Parish Meeting at the School was called. A surveyor from the RDC attended to give his opinion and explained that there was insufficient pressure to allow the main to be tapped further.

Sam from Evesham, was a very observant man; he sank his well where a patch of clover was green all the summer. Water, he said, was rising out of the little school desks we were all cramped in. Sam was bearded, rosy cheeked and dressed in his best jacket and corduroy trousers. He towered above most of us, being six foot three when he was an upright soldier in the Boer War. 'Thur's plenty of water at Paris, it just wants harnessing,' he said. 'If we could only harness it, get a ram and push it up into the plain by the Cuckoo Pen on Little Hill and build a reservoir, we'd 'ave enough pressure to supply all the houses in Ashton.'

Little Mr Penny, a gentleman gardener, then mentioned a spring running to waste on the Leasow further up the hill which would supply us by gravitation.

'Thee sit down, Master Penny,' said Sam. 'Thee hasn't bin yur long enough in the village to get thee seat warm. Thy logic ain't worth a hatful of crabs.'

Tom Wheatcroft, sitting sideways in the desk by me, whispered, 'Frederick, thee ut understand one day. Sam and Penny aren't first cousins (the best of friends). Master Penny bought a Model T Ford yesterday, and Sam called him a hungry gutted toad and that he ud yut and yut till he bursts.'

The RDC stated that the water up on the Leasow would be insufficient if we had a dry summer. Joe Baker, water diviner, disputed this and told us how many thousands of gallons ran to waste through the sheep-wash pool. This, he said, went underground for some distance and boiled up again by Shaw Green.

'I can prove it,' he said, 'I took some permanganate of potash and put a good doing in the Leasow spring and ran down to Shaw Green; the water was running out into that stream the colour of port wine.'

But the surveyor was not interested. This water would have supplied the top of the village, independent of the council main. That was what we wanted, to be independent.

The noisy, unruly meeting, chaired admirably by William Bostock, was told by the surveyor that a connection could be made to the main pipe at the next village, but the council-house rent and rates would be increased by at least half-a-crown a week to pay for it.

Dad said that the houses were built for the landworkers and he wanted their opinion. As one man, they said that half-a-crown a week was more than they could afford and they were satisfied.

That evening, as Dad sided with the low-paid landworkers, he found for the first time that he had offended some of the council tenants. I was proud of Dad. He didn't forget the old days when his parents had to scrape a living, when if his crippled mother's cat strayed after rabbits in the adjoining field, it would be shot.

These meetings were places where people could air their views perhaps bottled up for months previously. I remember one list of complaints: 'That thur hedge in the Chapel Orchard is right over the footpath up Holcombe Lane and scratts Master Whitfield's bus every time he goes up there. It a bin brought up now for three years at least, can't anything be done about it? Then thurs the Station Bridge – as slick as a glass bottle. All right for you gentlemen with cars but a devilishly ackud for me and my pony and trap. Get the clerk to write to the Company.' (The railway was always 'The Company'.)

I think that one must admit the average old-time countryman spoke his mind. It was quite common for one to say to another next day in the street, 'What I said last night was not to offend, although I knows you thinks different.'

'That's all right,' would come the reply, 'We beun't a goin to fall out over things like that.' One thing I learnt at these gatherings was that if something was said that 'reached you', as the saying is, it was unwise to lose your temper; much better to treat it lightly.

10

Recreation

TOYS AND GAMES

In an age when Woolworths had not reached Evesham, the only shops where we bought the raw materials for our toys were the Penny Bazaar and Mr Coombs'. Here, catapult elastic was sold by the yard, and if the hollow elder stick was not very effective, Mr Coombs' pea-shooters, at either a penny or a halfpenny each, were the answer. No, we didn't buy peas. The round variety known as Telegraph were good ammunition, easy to come by each February when the two-hundredweight sacks stood on the headland of the pea field and cousin George steered the drill up and down the rows.

When the March winds blew clouds of dust up our village street a few years before the tar came to bind the road surface, crazes started. There would be a craze for tops when, from Piggy Lane to Shepherd Corbisley's cottage, village boys took advantage of the hour of light left after tea to whip tops up and down the street as the farm men scuffed tiredly home from work.

But crazes lasted just a few weeks and then another one arrived in the playground of the lane and field. Our hoops were from the farmyard, not the town shops. Seed drills and horseshoes often lay abandoned among the hemlock and nettles of the rickyard when they wore out or got broken beyond repair. The wheels, about eighteen inches in diameter, were made of half-inch round iron. The wooden spokes and hubs when they rotted away left us hoops better than the flimsy wooden ones of the shops.

To run after an iron hoop down the hill of the village street and race against each other was great fun. But we found that by taking a piece of iron and persuading Caleb, the blacksmith, to turn the end into a hook on his anvil after heating it in the fire we had a hoop stick which made it easy to set the pace of the hoop rather than the hoop setting the pace for us.

Pop-guns, catapults and slings stayed with us throughout the year. Slings were made with a piece of soft leather from an old glove, cut with a pocket knife to about twice the size of a match box, then stitched at both ends so

Ashton village schoolchildren. The two boys in uniform are Dr Overthrow's sons

that two lengths of binder twine could be threaded through. Slings proved to be dangerous as we swung them loaded with a pebble around over our heads and released the one string. We rarely hit the target.

Pop-guns were harmless, innocent fun. At the back of our privy, or 'petty' as Dad called it, the elder bushes, or ellun, grew tall. Elder sticks with the pith gouged out with my pocket knife and the poker made a pop-gun barrel. The nut bushes grew as they always grew by the path side to the privy. The plunger for the pop-gun I made, as generations before had made them, from a fairly thick nut stick whittled down with the pen-knife until it was exactly like the inside of a bicycle pump with a similar handle. It had to fit the ellun barrel exactly to force air through. Ammunition lay close by, the pith from the bored-out elder stick rammed into the barrel; with practice the gun shot with a loud pop.

No one ever told me that to shoot at birds with a pebble from a catapult was cruel. It was the accepted thing to do, and why should I, at eight years old, question it. There was a code of conduct when bird-nesting that we only took one egg from a nest if we hadn't got that particular egg. Neither did we rob the nest of a sitting bird. The stalking of wild life has been the way man sustained his own life over the centuries. This maxim did not apply to me but was inherent in me. The satisfaction which came when first

I was able to bring home a rabbit for dinner killed with my own catapult! I'll never forget a catapult made from a forked stick, the elastic from Mr Coombs' shop bound on by thread from Mother's work-box. The leather which held the stone was just made from an old glove.

Oliver made me a tip-cat. A simple toy, just a nut stick about six inches long pointed at both ends by his draw shave in his vice. Placing it flat on a level road the two ends were about an inch from the ground. Just a smart tap with another stick about eighteen inches long made the tip-cat jump vertically in front of me and with practice the missile went flying through the air fifty yards or more.

When I think of freedom, my mind goes back to the Nap, or Knolp as the old folk called it. This part of Bredon has such a varied history; for generations, stone for the roads was quarried from the flat, but the southerly slope was a playground for children. On this slope grew a wiry type of grass, very slippery to climb when the sun had baked the underlying clay to a hard pan in the height of summer. Rough sledges were made by us boys out of old cider barrels and during the holidays we careered at terrific speed down the slope from the quarry on the top, then past the two coppices, the primrose coppice and violet coppice, until we reached a row of withies at the foot and by careful manoeuvring landed safely on the bridle road.

Up alongside Holcombe Nap was the primrose coppice where the ash poles grew on stools, or 'stowls' as the locals called them. These were lopped about every seven years to provide fencing materials, stakes and rails and were also used for hurdle-making.

The bigger boys of the village searched the coppice for poles for stilts. The art of finding suitable poles was inborn, like their fathers' skill when they looked for a scythe-handle or sned. The required stilt depended for its length, of course, on the height of the boy. The step to stand on was formed by lopping off most of a branch growing at a right angle to the main pole. It was a sight, an unforgettable sight, to see a dozen village lads walking hedge-high down our village streets on a spring or summer evening. Of course, some fell off while learning, but later they raced each other from Bakers Lane to the village Cross. You could buy gaudy painted stilts in the town shops with the foot rests screwed on to a straight stick, but these were 'boughten', as the old folk said, and boughten cake was frowned upon.

The sound of a cricket ball on a willow bat has been heard in the village for centuries. We made our own willow bats to play cricket on the short cropped grass of the footpath to Paris across Church Close. We climbed the willows before they were pollarded and cut with a hatchet a sizeable pole, then split it in half with wooden wedges hammered in with an old gate hook. The laborious task then began. After the required length of split willow came the whittling away at one end to form a handle. It took lots of patience and pocket knives to create a bat. Wickets were no problem at all; bundles of rick pegs lay about the farm.

When I was five the moat froze over, the big boys made a slide from the churchyard wall to the end where the moor-hens would nest later on. As the large pond was lit with stable lanterns at night, Dad took us up there to see Ralph Baker and Percy Wigley skate figures of eight on the ice. Boys and girls played hockey with a pebble and bent withy sticks.

And so with hide-and-seek in the hay tallet, or loft, over the stable, Saturday morning paper-chases or fox and hounds over Bredon Hill, boys and girls had little to desire in the way of simple sport. A 'Do-It-Yourself' project, when even the slide down the straw rick cost nothing.

It seemed a pity to me that it had to be spoiled by school in the week and Chapel on Sundays.

VILLAGE CRICKET

Our village, being a relatively poor one, was later than some in playing organised cricket. There was no half-day holiday on Saturdays eighty years ago for landworkers.

When Ashton Club was set up in 1907, there was soon trouble between Arthur Jackson, the vice-captain, and Fred Beasley, the big farmer who let the ground to the club. It had nothing to do with cricket, Arthur Jackson's cattle had broken through into Fred Beasley's mowing grass, but Mr Beasley barred Arthur from playing on his ground. For three years, Ashton Club and Arthur's own United Cricket Club were 'at loggeryuds', as Charlie Bradfield put it. Then the peace was made between the committees by Mr James Cambridge who had recently come to live in the village.

After this troublesome start, the club went from strength to strength and reached its heyday in the twenties when Mr Howard Cambridge, the son of the president, was captain and, with the aid of an excellent groundsman, produced a wicket near the station which was the talk of the district. High scores were commonplace; the outfield was as good as the square.

Old-time umpires were a law unto themselves and Lofty Summers was no exception. Ashton were playing Dumbleton and the last pair were batting for the visitors when Harry Shakespeare, Ashton's fast bowler, bowled a yorker. The Dumbleton batsman, playing with his bat and pad

Ashton-under-Hill Cricket Club

close together, edged the ball with his bat on to his pad. Lofty shouted, 'Out!'

'How can he be out?' the Ashton captain said. 'There's been no appeal and he played the ball with his bat.'

Lofty was unmoved. 'The ball hit him on the leg and anyroad I wants my tay and he's out.' Whether this affected the result of the match, I can't say, but it was an unusual decision. A visiting team from the other side of the hill were playing on our home ground and their umpire with his white smock and his pipe appeared to be watching the game but one appeal brought the reply, 'Not out, but if it occurs again it will be, to an appeal for lbw.'

Howard Cambridge, a keen cricketer and a good sport (he encouraged us boys), wanted a blacksmith to work on his farm to shoe and do repairs. He put an advertisement in the local paper for a blacksmith, preferably one who could play cricket. Whether Caleb Batchelor had ever handled a cricket bat before no one will ever know, but he was a useful blacksmith and turned out for the team on the Saturday.

146

I shall never forget him. He wore white flannels but with broad braces and a leather belt with a huge brass buckle. His arms were like legs of mutton, well tattooed, and as he waddled out to bat at about number eight the locals were wondering how he would shape. I think the team was Alcester and Ragley, one of the best teams we played. Caleb took centre for the first ball from their fast bowler. He ran up the pitch, turned a well-pitched ball on the off into a full toss and sent it to the square leg boundary as if he was hitting the anvil. His sledge-hammer strokes produced the runs and the better the ball, the harder he thumped it. Straight drives went to long on and agricultural strokes to leg. After he had made fifty he was caught out on the square leg boundary, but he had played himself into the team. I suppose that after a day swinging a sledge-hammer this was child's play to Caleb.

He made history in our village when he hit a six over the scoring hut; it landed at Gloucester twenty miles away. The ball landed in an open railway truck as a goods train passed through the station and was found when the train stopped at Gloucester.

As well as the sloggers, we had also some classical batsmen. Gordon Johnson was as fast a bowler as we had, an excellent slip fielder and a batsman who played all the strokes in the book. The week after he gained his county cap he turned out for the village team. He batted in that honoured place, first wicket down, and as he came down our pavilion steps, immaculate in his Gloucestershire cap, we schoolboys sitting on the grass by the red withy tree thought we were in for a treat. He walked out to his crease and one or two gentlemen with cigars clapped him as he took middle and leg. The first ball well on the leg side he padded up to in the orthodox county style. The umpire at the other end sitting on his shooting stick, after an appeal by the bowler, raised the dreaded finger and Gordon Johnson was on his way back to the pavilion. Old Charlie Bradfield said, 'Oi, Gordon used a word when he went up them pervilion steps as yunt in the prayer book. Looks bad, ya know, when he had bin a-playing for the county. But I'll tell tha what it is, Fred, thee never wants to let that ball hit yer pads when old so-and-so's a-empiring. You'll be out else.'

Around the scoring hut a group of youths lazed on the grass and put the numbers of every ten runs that were scored or when a wicket fell. If someone was out for a duck, or a quack, a rather nicely white-painted duck on the metal square was pegged on the board.

Howard Walsey was a regular umpire and had a little wire-haired fox terrier named Nip, who lay on the grass by the scoring hut while Howard was busy umpiring. The lads tied a tin-square duck on Nip's collar, and after Nip had circled the boundary he went to his master at the wicket. By this time the culprits had fled into Catherine's Meadow as Howard chased them waving his shooting stick.

FOOTBALL – THE ASHTON TIGERS

As far as I can gather, football was played in our village in the 1890s but it was not until the 1920s that our team, The Tigers, became famous for miles around. Earlier teams had played in the New Piece but the team in the twenties played in the Wynch, that level piece of turf which was just over the stile from our yard. Football in the Wynch brought most of the village out on Saturday afternoons. The Sedgeberrow supporters walked across the fields. As a small boy, I rarely missed a home game. My Aunt Annie knitted me a black and gold woollen mascot shaped like a tiger which I wore on the lapel of my mac.

Ashton-under-Hill Football Club. Stodge Warren is on the left-hand end of the back row

I remember Stodge, the roadman, who used to arrive early and hook the nets on the goal posts. He was a stocky, lame man who had led a varied life from poaching to driving steam-ploughing tackle. He carried a large jar of cider which, when he waddled, looked half as big as himself. He also brought with him a cider horn to tot out. The players who drank cider had some before the game and more at half-time when Stodge half ran and half walked into the field.

If a player got injured, two people rushed on to the field, the trainer Charlie Cuthbert, a ganger on the railway, and Stodge. Charlie attended the injured player, first with the magic sponge, smelling salts and liniment, home-made from eggs and turpentine. As he recovered, Stodge would pour the player out one little horn of cider. If a knee was dislocated, Joe Baker was called.

In their heyday, our village teams won the First Division, Cheltenham League, three years running, and the Cheltenham Hospital Cup.

We all had our idols; mine was Tosh Ballard on the left wing. Another favourite of mine was George Pearce, a right back. He lofted the ball up to the forwards almost in the goal mouth of our opponents, but when we were winning, say about three to one with ten minutes to play, he often skied the ball into Bowles' walnut tree and the visiting supporters shouted, 'Keep him on the island.' Amusing incidents on the Wynch there were plenty. Titch Pope was so drunk in one match he stayed offside and the Ref ignored him – a pity, we needed his skill and ball control. Our opponents were Bretforton's Old Boys, a strong team.

As a boy I never enjoyed Friendly matches – 'It's only a Friendly today, it won't be much of a game.' In a Friendly, there wasn't the full-blooded tackle or the charging of the goalkeeper (in order then).

On 9 November 1924, we were at home to Fairford Town in the North Gloucestershire Senior Cup. There were nearly one thousand spectators on the Wynch and they came by all means of transport and approached the ground through our horse road, past the granary and cow shed. Captain Barton, ex-Indian Army, was in goal and the atmosphere was electric when, with ten minutes to go in this important semi-final, the teams were drawing, one goal each. Suddenly, from a clearance by George Pearce to centre half Billy Stevens, Billy took a thirty yard shot at goal with terrific power. The Fairford goalie just couldn't stop this one – waist high, nearly in the corner of the net. Into the net it went, broke the net and went straight through, to be stopped by a small boy. The Ref, who was in mid-field, gave a goal kick, maintaining that the ball was wide of the post. Pandemonium broke out as the Ashton and Sedgeberrow women supporters threatened the Ref with umbrellas and sticks, but the Ref was adamant and Stodge mended the net with a piece of string out of his pocket saying, 'I'll see there won't be nair another gu through there.' His language was then not exactly drawing room and the Honorary Secretary, who also kept the churchyard tidy, said, 'Stodge, that's enough of that language in front of ladies.'

Stodge replied, primed with cider, 'Yer's the hook, (the hook used for putting the nets up), and I'll be gone and besides I've yerd thee swear many a time up in that churchyard.'

The match was a draw and Ashton lost the replay.

PUBS, NAOMI'S COTTAGE AND THE ROOM

Men who worked on the land all day sometimes needed an escape from the one-bedroomed cottages, where the fire was hidden by drying washing. In those days the pubs were a male preserve, the women's meeting place the village shop or the Post Office. There were two pubs, both selling farm cider and beer from local breweries. The Plough and Harrow was thatched and had a huge open fire and a painting of two labourers and their horses ploughing and harrowing. The Star I knew better as it was near our farm. Mr Collins the landlord was father-in-law to Mrs Collins who ran the shop; his wife was a kindly woman who came to our Chapel. The stone floor was partly covered by coconut matting, and there was a sawdust-filled iron spittoon in the middle of the bar, reached with unerring aim by the old men who chewed tobacco. Tobacco smoke mingled with the pungent smell of wet corduroys as the rain-sodden workers dried off by the parlour fire. In front of The Star was a thatched drink house, like a miniature cottage, where the beer was kept cool in summer.

The villagers also had a home-made consolation for hard lives. They made wine out of anything, recipes handed down, usually from mother to daughter as the winemakers were mostly women. Kate Dunn's beetroot wine equalled a good port, Millie Bostock's cowslip was as smooth as silk. The great thing about all this fermentation of fruit, flower and sugar was its unknown strength. Some home-made wine, which was just like drinking milk, was sly and got many a man in trouble with his family when he got home. Plum jerkum, that wine of the Pershore plum, can be very strong. It can have a quarrelsome effect on a man. In the cottages in those days glass

The Plough and Harrow pub at Ashton

The Star Inn, Ashton-under-Hill, here occupied by the Collins family

jars stood in the small windows behind the check curtains. Jars like large goldfish bowls where little bits of stuff like cotton wool rose and fell to the bottom of the jar. Known as bee wine, the bees having to be supposedly fed with sugar pretty often, the honey-coloured liquid fermented until when bottled it was sweet and, according to the strict chapel abstainers, non-alcoholic, but was it? It made many a countryman say more than his piece after dinner.

The village boys had an unofficial club at Naomi's Cottage. Naomi was bent and old, on two sticks, and had a hooked nose and one very long tooth. She looked like a witch, and had a grown-up son, a love-child, with the mind of a child. The fourteen-year-old village boys sat around her fire, drinking cocoa and smoking Woodbines at twopence for five. The old horned gramophone played *Ramona, How Long has this been going on, Horsey, cock yer tail up*, and the other current favourites which they took it in turns to buy. Sometimes Naomi's son would bring them cider from the farm where he worked, and would toast them rounds of bread at the fire. When they were sixteen they were old enough to go to the Room of an evening.

The Room, or Recreation Room, a wooden army hut from the First World War, was a social centre for the village. Here the click of billiard balls could be heard as they crossed the bright green baize under the powerful Aladdin lamps. The shirt-sleeved youths of the village vied with their elders chalking the cue, potting the red. The billiard table, a present from Sir James Cosnett who gained his title through his efforts in equalling out the food for the Midland counties during the war, was full size on huge bulbous legs. Visitors to the village, were amazed at its perfection. Others played quoits or dominoes, or learnt how to box with the custodian, Reggie Parminter, an ex-naval man.

But as few villages had such social centres, how did this place under Bredon get theirs? Mr Cambridge gave it, his father paid to have it erected by a local firm of builders. The building chaps were very thirsty that hot summer in the 1920s. Ponto carried cider with a yoke and two buckets from Dunn's and they drank it as fast as he carried it. In between times he did carry water to mix the cement mortar for the brick piers. Our Room was built on cider.

Other attractions or distractions at 'The Room' were Mothers' Union teas and whist drives. These were conducted with immense respectability. The Room trustees had made a rule that no intoxicating liquor was ever to enter the premises. Here the Chapel and the pubs were at one. The Chapel welcomed this because of its principles, the pubs because it would lose them no trade. So at weddings if the couple were toasted in champagne, it had to be at the school. Only the odd Chapel goer went to the whist drives, the majority believing that the hearts, clubs, diamonds and spades were the works of the devil. Church folk went, but there was no whist playing during Lent, no dancing either, just at the time of year when folk needed something to cheer them up after the winter and before the spring.

About twice every winter we had a magic lantern lecture in 'The Room'. There was no radio then and no possibility of a visit to the pictures so these lectures were an interlude in the humdrum of school, work and bed. The magic lantern belonged to Mr Robert Cambridge and, of course, was a carbide model. Some returned missionary would arrive with the slides and erect the screen in 'The Room'. 'Seven-thirty tonight,' read the posters, 'Mr Blank will show pictures and describe life in an outpost of the British Empire.'

At seven o'clock a few of us lads were looking through the windows of the Recreation Room while Percy Wigley helped Mr Howard Cambridge load the canister of the lantern with carbide and start the water dripping until a match lit the lantern and projected a yellowish light on to the screen. We filed into our seats at about seven-fifteen and sat in a group around the stove, partly because it was warm there and partly to be out of sight of the more serious-minded members who did not consider this as an entertainment but a lesson to us to appreciate the lovely surroundings we lived in under the hill.

The first hymn projected on the screen, *The Church's One Foundation*, I always suspected was to make both Church and Chapel feel at home. Then came the pictures. Bare-breasted women in straw skirts. The room was dark so that a giggle could not be traced to any one of us, but we were not accustomed to seeing things like this up our village street and giggle we did. They showed us men with bone skewers through their noses and sometimes the giraffe-necked women from Burma. No doubt the message was acceptable to the older members of the audience and we put our pennies in the collection, but to be honest it was the pictures we wanted and, though imperfect, they gave us something to talk about in the long dark winter. The lantern was usually reliable, but once we noticed more of a bubbling and gurgling coming from the canister holding the carbide. Then, all at once, the whole thing burst into flames right in the middle of *Greenland's Icy Mountains*, the last hymn to be projected on to the screen. Percy Wigley turned off the gas and no harm was done.

ARMISTICE TEA

As the dark winter evenings approached in our oil-lit village, the Armistice Tea in the Recreation Room was looked forward to by everyone. The main object of the tea was to show appreciation of the Ashton men who had fought in the 1914 war.

After the tea, the concert which followed was entirely impromptu. Reggie Parminter had spent the afternoon carrying water from the standpipe by the village Cross and waiting on the ladies who provided the tea. He lit the fire in the copper furnace and boiled the water for them, fetched the coal, trimmed the lamps and then, with the help of the porter from the station, fetched on a sack-cart the piano from the village school. The tea provided was the best of the year. Great hams and joints of beef were skilfully carved by Howard Cambridge, who had driven a Model T Ford in the Middle East. When Mr Cambridge Senior was well enough, he took the chair at the concert. Failing this, Dad took his place. There was a little business to attend to before the entertainment began. Someone had to be appointed to care for the War Memorial garden for the next year and Mr Penny was thanked by Dad, who was in the chair, for the way he had kept things tidy throughout the year. This was agreed by everyone except Joe Baker who said: 'When you be in the army they allus reckons to put the big soldiers at the back and the little chaps in front when drilling. Mr Penny has put little flowers at the back and these poor little fellows be trying their best to look over the heads of the big chaps at the front.' Mr Penny proposed that Joe Baker be appointed to look after the Memorial for the next year, which was lightheartedly agreed by everyone. In fact what happened was that they did the job together, being good gardeners and good friends.

The room was packed and the ex-servicemen, apart from having a free tea, were now handing the tobacco jar up and down the long trestle tables, filling their pipes full of tobacco and the room full of smoke. Others were content with a drag at a Woodbine, while Mr Cambridge Senior, when present, puffed at a Churchill-sized cigar. Mr Robert Cambridge, Howard's brother, opened the concert with a beautiful rendering of *The Londonderry Air* on his violin. He had difficulty in tuning it with the piano, the journey down the rough village street on the sack-cart had not done the piano any good. Joe Baker's daughter, Violet, an excellent pianist, skilfully covered up some of the piano's faults by putting in twiddly bits. Edgar Macormick, a handsome man immaculately dressed in a blue suit with a chalk stripe and smoking a Sarony in a long cigarette holder, I imagine made the hearts of some of the young ladies of our village miss at least one beat. He didn't speak in our local brogue but had a pleasant public school accent without being affected. Working in insurance, he had not experienced clay on his boots since leaving Flanders with a commission. His song, *The Gay Drum Major*, appealed to us boys. The ladies were touched by 'Now we all can understand why the darlings love the band, especially the gay drum major.'

Henry Watson, a fruit and vegetable merchant, originally a Black Country man, was well liked in our village. He was choirmaster at the Church and told some very good stories of the Black Country where everything revolved around the pub and the 'cut' (canal). Year by year, he sang *Trumpeter, what are you sounding now* in a very well-modulated voice, which almost dropped to a whisper at the last sad verse. Howard Cambridge cracked jokes in between the songs and recited some of his own composition. As Howard told us of the farmer's boy going for a job at Master Brown's and Master Brown saying, 'Why are you leaving Master Green's?', Shepherd Corbisley, sitting next to his wife by the piano and smoking his clay pipe, exploded with bronchial laughter before the end of the tale which he knew so well. 'I be leaving Master Green's,' said the boy, 'on account a' the fittle.'

'Rubbish,' said Master Brown. 'I know Master Green would give you ample to eat.'

'Oh, thur's plenty,' said the boy, 'but fust the old cow died and we yut her; then the old sow died and we yut her; then the old 'ooman died so I thought it was time to leave.' Then Mrs Collins from the shop sang *I'm following in Father's footsteps* in a Florrie Ford style.

The Recreation Room was warming up. The stove was red hot. Some of us went back-stage and helped to clear up the jellies and trifle; others slipped out and produced bottles of beer from under the steps which they drank under the walnut tree in the orchard.

We listened intently to the conversations of the ex-soldiers, tales of mud and rats. Then the chairman asked Ernest Bradfield the thatcher, if he could think of a song. We all knew what it would be. He didn't need the piano, so Violet had a rest. He stood against the trestle table dressed in his best navy-blue suit with his medals on his chest. He drew himself up to the six foot two he was and then put the thumb of his right hand down under his broad leather belt and moved the big brass buckle slightly to one side. Clearing his throat, his eyes firmly fixed on the rafters above him, he sang with feeling:

'If those lips could only speak
And those eyes could only see
From the beautiful picture
In the beautiful golden frame.'

As he put the feeling and the tragedy into those old words, hearts were stirred and memories revived of men the village people had known and loved, but who had failed to return in 1918. Dad now asked if we could all sing *Just a song at twilight when the lights are low*, his favourite. The evening was going, slipping away too fast for a schoolboy. This was the night we learned more about people we had only seen at work in the fields, hedging, gate-hanging, fruit picking.

Walt, our carter, needed a lot of persuasion to do his bit. With a certain lilt in his voice, as if he were ploughing a lonely hillside, he sang unaccompanied.

Mr Penny, a useful tenor, didn't trust the piano and brought his tuning fork with him. He struck this on his knee and repeated, 'Doh, doh, doh,' until he was satisfied he had the right note. He gave us *Santa Lucia* with credit. More doh, doh, doh on the tuning fork and Mr Penny continued, asking the company to join in with *The March of the Cameron Men* and *The Campbells are coming*.

Joe Baker, the man of so many parts, gave an exhibition with the bones and recited *The hen that laid astray*.

'What about you, Shepherd?' Dad said, as Shepherd Corbisley was enjoying a clay pipe of Red Bell tobacco. 'I got it on my chest tonight, Master,' he said. But with a prod from his wife he sang a couple of songs between little choking coughs.

When the village baker, as good-humoured a man as ever went to a party, sang his songs with a twinkle in his eye, we were all silent in case we missed any words which he sang at a rare speed. He was the salt of the earth, a man who found time for everybody, even us lads, and our favourite song of his was:

'John Brown he had a party
On Tuesday of last week;
Tom Biggs was there as usual
With all his sauce and cheek.
He said, "You chaps, I just have pinched
A sovereign from a pal.

156

Shall we have smokes and drinks with it?"
I said, "Of course we shall."
We had whiskeys round and ninepenny smokes
And quite enjoyed the spree,
We laughed, we roared, we chuckled aloud with glee.
We screamed, we howled, we thought the joke was fine.
I didn't know till afterwards the quid was mine.'

John Harris, bass, painter and decorator, was all the time getting his strength up behind the stage, clearing up the ham and beef sandwiches which were left on the billiard table and swilling them down with cups of stewed black tea out of the two tea urns which stood by the copper boiler. As he poured himself a cup he was humming a few tunes to himself awaiting his turn to be accompanied by Violet Baker on the school piano. Like a real old trouper he made his entry past the big guns of our village, who were sitting at the top table, to be introduced properly as John Harris, bass. He was dressed in a morning suit of sorts with cloth-covered buttons, his starched shirt front partly hidden by a blue and white spotted cravat. He put a whole bale of music, yellow with age, on top of the piano and we looked like being there all night. Just what I wanted. He waded through one piece after another, reaching deep notes I never thought were possible. He was a bass all right. 'Would you like a little jelly?' suggested Mrs Collins from the shop. 'Indeed, I would, Mam,' John said, and Violet had a breather while John Harris cleared up half a bowl of raspberry jelly, the stuff just melting as the dessert spoon entered his mouth, particles clinging for a moment to his tobacco-stained walrus moustache. How long John would have sung we shall never know, for after about half an hour of these ballads of love and passion the chairman called a halt and with *Auld Lang Syne* and *The King* sung by all, the party was over.

A VILLAGE FÊTE IN THE 1920s

When money had to be raised in our village, the committee (we loved forming committees) decided on a fête. The locals never did understand the circumflex *e* and these functions were known as 'feets'. 'Bist a goin to the feet?' old Frank Wheatcroft would ask me as I walked up the Groaten from the four-ten train from school. 'It's tomorrow, Saturday, as ever was,' he went on, 'and Sir James is opening it from the cricket pavilion.'

'I know, Frank, I've got to present him with a buttonhole, carnations, I think.'

157

'Bunty pulls the string' at a village fête

'Well, thee ull manage that bit of a job surely?' he said.

That Friday evening the cricket ground was a hive of activity. The fête was for the Cricket Club. The stalls were both numerous and varied. The evergreen hoop-la was being erected, a stall was run by a buxom farmer's wife, whose son had already been through all the cigarette packets (some of the prizes) and taken out the fag cards. This gave him an unfair advantage over me. Another circular tent top of pink and white covered a table stacked with toys, trinkets and all the odd things people give for these affairs. Every parcel had a long string on it which reached outside the stall. 'Bunty pulls the string' was placarded on cardboard on the top of the tent pole. By paying threepence or sixpence you were allowed to pull the string and as the showman said 'a prize every time, lady'.

Mrs Hunter, part gipsy, one of the travelling type, had brought her donkeys over from the other side of the hill and gave donkey rides for children at sixpence a time alongside the wire fence which separated the cricket ground from the Naits. The Naits had not been mown and the mowing grass here was rank and tall with meadowstreet and cow parsley.

Saturday morning, after the mist along the brookside and a drenching dew on the grass, promised to be hot and fine and we were not to be disappointed. A horse and dray of Howard Cambridge's was being driven by his carter, old Jimmy Blizzard. He was loaded with trestles and tables for the teas, then he fetched the coconut shy to be erected against the back of an old cowshed where the horse-drawn cricket roller and mower were kept. Howard Cambridge had an idea that, to be different, we would throw rick pegs at the coconuts instead of the usual balls; this proved quite successful, the coconuts falling more by luck than judgment. By three o'clock everyone was assembled by the pavilion. The Ashton Cricket Club flag – yellow and navy, the same colours as the football team jerseys (the Tigers) – was fluttering in the slight breeze. Sir James and Lady Cosnett were both on the steps for the opening ceremony, supported by Mr Cambridge Senior, the Vicar and, in fact, all the upper class we could muster. Sir James was a very ordinary sort of man, 'No side on him,' Tom Wheatcroft confided to me, 'thee hast no cause to be nervous of him, nor his missus, they be just like one a we.' Edna Collins, the shopkeeper's daughter, was about a year younger than me and she had been chosen to present Lady Cosnett with a bouquet as soon as the fête was officially opened. Edna – shortish, plump with puppy fat – walked up as gracefully as she could in her pink crêpe de Chine dress ornamented with rosebuds, curtsied and gave her bouquet to Lady Cosnett. Then came my turn just as the clapping died down for Edna. I had been smartened up no end by Mother and had plastered Jockey Club on my fair hair which actually had a parting. As I gave Sir James his buttonhole, expecting to make a hasty retreat, he grabbed me by the hand and said what a smart young fellow I was and hoped that one day I would be playing for the village cricket team (this I did some years later). The fête was under way.

A railway ganger who was staying in the next village brought with him a 'shocking coil' – an electrical device that sent pins and needles up the arm by holding the two terminals from the battery and which was supposed to cure rheumatism. He placed the two leads in a bucket of water, put half-a-crown in the bottom and charged twopence a go to get the half-crown. I saw lots of people in all sorts of contortions but the electric shock in the water just wouldn't allow time to grab the half-crown. As I stood there about tea-time, Jim Bradfield, had a go and much to everyone's delight retrieved the prize.

It is surprising how ingenious people can get when they put heart and soul into an effort to raise money for a good cause. Howard Cambridge gave one of his best weaner pigs for a competition. The people who took part had to nurse the pig, keep it quiet and sing a song in front of the crowd without laughing. One after another tried and the pig squealed and the crowd laughed and the competitors, laughing themselves, gave up. Mrs Hunter was game to make an honest copper, as she said. She nursed the pig in her apron, stood on the pavilion steps and gently rocked it like nursing a baby until it was almost sleeping and sang,

> 'The tears rolled down in her sun burnt cheeks,
> And dropped on the letter in her hand.
> Is it true, too true, more trouble in our native land. . .'

She sang without batting an eyelid. She looked dead serious as the pig was spending a penny and soaking her apron. The crowd was almost hysterical with laughter. Mrs Hunter won the pig – she won other pigs at other fêtes – and deserved it.

At every fête someone has to tell fortunes. Evangeline Agg, a farmer's daughter ('a fine piece', Frank described her. 'Her looks all right when 'ers got up for fox hunting, mind'), pitched her tent under the withies not far from where Reggie Parminter was boiling the water in a copper for the tea. We helped Reggie to gather wood to stoke the copper boiler and the ladies made the tea.

Evangeline was dressed as a gipsy. This was not awfully difficult; she had raven black hair, about thirtyish, Frank reckoned she was, and she had an olive complexion. She wore a coloured scarf over her head, two enormous earrings, bangles, and no stockings which Frank said made her a bit gallus. From the bottom of her red dressing gown, she showed a pair of fancy garters. Two chairs were placed either side of the table in the tent and a crystal ball shone like a diamond on the green baize of the card table. She did very good business all day. 'I be goin' to have me bob's worth,' old Frank told me, 'if it's only to hold hands with her for a few minutes.' We boys peeped under the canvas and listened to what she told her clients.

The sun had gone down over Bredon Hill, the dew was rising and most of us were gone home, but Frank Wheatcroft had to stay to help Jimmy Blizzard load the trestle tables and clear up the stalls, the next day being Sunday. 'Thee ut remember Evangeline a forchun telling,' he asked me on the Monday morning.

'Yes, what about it? She did very well for the club, didn't she?'

'Oi her did,' Frank said, 'and her didn't do so bad after the feet.'

'What happened, Frank? Nothing bad, I hope?'

'Well, yes and no,' Frank said. 'You remember the gentleman from Beckford a comin' about tay-time?'

'Yes,' I said.

'Well,' said Frank, 'this is the sarten truth as I be tellin' ya. Me and Jimmy had a squint in that tent just at the edge a night, so to speak, and he was a telling Evangeline's fortune in there. If thee dostn't know what I means you ul one day.'

I had a good idea what Frank meant. He talked in riddles but we were all used to it.

The fête was a great success, as they usually were, but about a fortnight later I had been helping Tom Wheatcroft to move some weaner calves from the long shed into the lidded place, and I caught ringworm from them, one on my arm and another in the parting of my hair. Nothing unusual, but Edna Collins started ringworm at the same time. Didn't old Tom tease me! 'What was thee and Edna at in that rank mowing grass full o' meadowsweet? Old Jimmy Blizzard a just told me that when he mowed it, it was beat down terrible by the fence t'other side of the coconut shies, some young uns had bin a rompin' there. It's no good a saying it wasn't thee and Edna, Frederick, cos you was sin.' That took a long time to live down.

OUTINGS AND THE VILLAGE BUS

In the 1920s and early 1930s when the workers on the land had no paid holidays except perhaps Christmas Day and Good Friday, the villagers who ventured to the seaside were few and far between. Jim, Dunn's under-carter, who started at nine shillings a week, had sixpence pocket money. He made a point of asking Mr Dunn to include at least one sixpence in his wage packet. How did Jim budget his weekly pocket money? First of all he had a sit-up-and-beg lady's bike which took him to Evesham on Sunday after-noons. It was threepence to hire a punt on the Avon, twopence to buy five Woodbines, which left Jim with enough to buy a pennyworth of chips. Sometimes he did have a little overtime money, but that was Jim's weekly break from work.

The little crocodile of country folk who dared to break the Sabbath and take advantage of the four shillings half-day trip to Weston-super-Mare could be seen walking with carrier bags of sandwiches, bottles of tea, down the Groaten to the railway station. When one thinks of poverty in the country, it's natural to think of the last century, but the scheming and scraping of our villagers of sixty years ago must not be forgotten.

A local family all dressed up ready for an outing to Weston-super-Mare. Stodge Warren is wearing an engine driver's cap

It's true there were compensations for the thirty-shillings-a-week man – his cheap house, his potatoes, land and garden, fruit, rabbits and so on – but hard cash was scarce and the Friday night's packet was divided on the kitchen table like a packet of sweets to a family of children. To see families walking the country lanes on summer Sunday evenings, or blackberrying on the Hill, the children gathering dandelions for their tame rabbits, was a piece of life in the country not easily forgotten.

When the Chapel organised the Sunday School outing, the collection from the Anniversary Service paid for the children to go to Weston or Malvern by train. Parents who had saved a bit of overtime money made it a day out. The Midnight Milkman came with Sacco to Weston and once never saw the sea, spending the whole day in a pub. Tea on the Grand Pier was a never-to-be-forgotten luxury. Then the older men with pancake cap, best dark tweed suit with trousers rolled up to the knee, heavy boots slung with their leather laces across the shoulders, paddled in the muddy sea.

Visits to Malvern with tea at Dorothy's café meant changing trains at Ashchurch and then on to the old Malvern line. The blind man played his melodeon at St Anne's Well. The cooling spring water was drunk from cupped hands by the Sunday School boys. While the young people climbed to the summit to view the pastoral counties of the middle west, their elders dozed on the seats a little way above the town, looking forward to Dorothy's café.

Roadmen, for reasons we never knew, always had a shilling or so above the agricultural rate. They even had a day's holiday with pay at times. Before the county councils made themselves responsible for all the roads, the village roads and byroads were under the care of the Rural District Council. Evesham Rural District Council, a neighbouring authority to Pershore, organised a 'Roadmen's Outing'. The destination was Southend. So picks and shovels and brooms and bagging hooks were put aside for a day at the sea. The Great Western train left early from Pershore and Evesham stations *en route* for London.

The day trip was well patronised by the roadmen of the villages. They looked somehow out of place on the London train with their tweed jackets, flannel trousers, cord waistcoats and their caps and straw hats. As Spider told a businessman on the train, the surveyor wouldn't give a man a job unless the skin on the palm of his hands was hard and gnarled with work. 'Nor if he wears a collar and tie. It must be a muffler in winter and a collarless shirt in summer. We beunt what they call white-collared workers.'

After walking the shingle, viewing the pier, eating cockles off the stalls, fish and chips swilled with vinegar, and drinking beer, Stodge and Spider sat on the sunny beach, their caps pulled over their eyes and slept the afternoon away.

The journey home from Southend started without incident. At London, when the party came up from the depths of the tube to see Piccadilly and were allowed two hours to see the sights, roadmen went in all directions. Stodge and Spider kept together. 'We wants to ketch the train to Evesham and be there on time.'

At the appointed time Spider and Stodge boarded the train for Evesham with just a sprinkling of the men who had started on the trip. The foreman counted and recounted the men and was worried about the ones left behind. Late that memorable night, phones were ringing in the villages of the Vale from the men who had missed the connection.

That Sunday the men who worked on our village roads were arriving home in all sorts of ways. Some got the Cheltenham train and walked eleven to sixteen miles home, arriving about Sunday dinner time. Another party hitched a ride from a lorry going to Worcester, and two took a taxi all the way from London. The details of the outing never got in the paper and it was a sore point with the local roadmen for years.

Uncle George Archer standing in front of the twelve-seater Brown Eagle; the Ashton village bus

When the old cinema closed in Swan Lane, Evesham, the Scala was built in the High Street. During the day we were served by trains on the branch line, but George Anderson, motor engineer who at one time drove steamers on the Avon, now saw possibilities in providing a village bus. His first effort was a Model T Ford which he converted from a lorry to a covered vehicle with benches both sides and a step at the back. The seating was for about eight, but it took more as he started for town at six o'clock on those Saturday nights, coming back when the pictures were over. This provided a long-felt want for the young folk, who could now sit on the plush seats of the Scala to watch Charlie Chaplin and *The Kid*, Mary Pickford and Douglas Fairbanks, while the little orchestra in front of the screen played suitable music and the drums rolled and the cymbals clanged at the vital moments. Soon the talkies came and they enjoyed the love scenes, aware that the Elders of the Chapel would be appalled at the low-cut bodices and stories of unfaithfulness.

During the day and in the week the Model T went to town with shoppers, loaded at the back end with small market gardeners' produce and returning with the empty hampers.

But the Model T was fast becoming too small for the villagers, and to everybody's surprise the local paper one Friday ran a story entitled 'Built in a Bedroom'. George Anderson had made a bus partly in a bedroom in his house. In no time at all it was on the road, the Brown Eagle, a twelve seater with the seats comfortably upholstered by Mrs Anderson, matching curtains, a luxury bus for that time. By shoving up a bit, a twelve-seater could hold far more on a Saturday night, and was packed to the door; one could hear in there all the local news without buying a paper. 'Mrs So-and-so is having another babby.' 'That ull be five, won't it, Mrs Jones?. . .' 'Gunner's peas av all bin utt by the jackdaws. . . .' 'My Lord, old Master Dunn as lived here yers ago, father of the one at the farm, left a smart bit a money. . . .' 'I say, that's a nice bit a mate from Byrds, unt it?. . .' George Anderson puffed at his pipe, dropped passengers at their doors. To say he was responsible for many marriages and births would be true, but deaths, no, because over the years from the Model T to the Brown Eagle, George always got his passengers home safely. He no doubt heard more village talk on those Saturday nights than in the barber's shop.

*

CHRISTMAS, BOXING DAY
AND NEW YEAR'S EVE

My first recollections of Christmas were the bells ringing before daybreak on 21 December, St Thomas's morning, and the little boys singing in the half-light, 'Here we come a-Thomasin', a-Thomasin', a-Thomasin', Here we come a-Thomasin', so early in the morning.' They were singing for pennies.

What of Christmas Day for us? Sugar mice in our stockings. Sucking pig for dinner. The flocks of carol singers. A sack bag of oranges in the hall to give them. Christmas puddings hooked out by the string from our copper boiler, using a toasting fork. The smell of steam. The size of the raisins. On Christmas afternoon we had a visit from the Tewkesbury Drum and Fife Band. I was fascinated with this and Tom Wheatcroft, who was with the cows in the yard, about to milk or 'draw the blessing', as he called it, said, 'Oi, we a got the tabber and tut come agun.' The wind howled up our chimney as the kettle swung on the pot hook over our oven grate in the kitchen one Christmas and Dad remarked how bad it was for those at sea. Then he told us of big freeze ups when a pig was roasted on the frozen Avon at Evesham and Grandfather Westwood skated to Tewkesbury. Men could tag on behind the threshing drum from farm to farm if they were lucky and provided their own shuppick (fork). Some took to poaching; some sold herrings, walking around the villages. We felt thankful for a good roof and plenty of little luxuries.

Boxing Day was a grand shooting day for us. The rabbits caught were sent to Evesham Workhouse to give the inmates rabbit pie suppers. I recall one such day on the hill, when some of Mr Carter's and Dad's friends from Evesham kept up a continual barrage. The cartridges, Crimson Flash, came in hundreds from Barrats, near Evesham river bridge. I was lucky to escape worse when one stray pellet ricocheted off a stone wall and drilled a hole through the top of my ear. After we had changed we all went to Mr Carter's to a lovely tea, chocolate blancmange with a lion on the top of the mould, lots of trifle, jellies of all flavours and pink celery. Mr Carter grew some crisp pink celery which was rather noisy as we sat around his big dining table eating it. The tea was strong and I liked it that way. I believe Mr Carter bought it in bulk in chests. He was the sort of man who bought in bulk: trucks of coal at the station, soap in large quantities and huge blocks of salt. He thought big and he bought big. After the usual crackers we played 'Pit', a game which can get very noisy. Miss Carter's young man got very boisterous as he shouted, 'Come on Barley.'

Mr Carter had laid by a good stock of walnuts off the five trees in his rickyard and with a brass top we played 'Put and take' for them. It doesn't sound very Chapel but I won a lot of walnuts one Christmas, though it didn't start me backing horses. Uncle Jim said, when he could see the bookmakers walking the roads with the seat out of their trousers and the backers driving their posh cars, he'd think there was something in it.

At about seven o'clock on Boxing Night the Evesham Salvation Army Band formed up on Mr Carter's lawn. Both he and Dad had been in the band and made them welcome. I don't honestly think there are many things more stirring than to hear the Army play carols on a clear, crisp, frosty night. We stood on the front steps, the acetylene lamp hanging from a pole in the midst of the group, and heard the familiar old tunes, 'Who is he in yonder stall?' What would Christmas have been without it?

Back in the drawing room Mr Carter had put the butt of a hawthorn tree on the open fire. As we sat snugly round and carried on eating the mince pies, the band left. Dad said to Mr Carter, 'Do you remember that winter, Harry, when we were out playing carols with the band?'

The Salvation Army band. Tom Archer is on the right with his euphonium

'Yes, Tom, I do, and it almost froze our breath that night. Instruments, Tom! I had to keep a bar of soap in my tunic pocket to fill the holes up in my euphonium, but we were about forty strong then.'

We left Mr Carter's at about eight-thirty and were in our kitchen at home getting ready for bed when a knock came at the door and Walt in a stage whisper enquired, 'Be the little uns gone to bed?' The bell ringers had arrived and we were not in bed. 'Shall we sing you a couple of carols, Mam?'

Mother said, 'Certainly, Walt. Having a good Christmas?'

Walt said, 'Oi, but I ca'unt sing like I used to years agu.' By the light of Walt's stable lantern hung on a forked stick, the five ringers started. Job Wheatcroft on crutches (he'd lost a leg at Mons) gave the note. He had a deep bass voice. They sang, *All Hail and Praise, the Sacred Morn,* then *Arise, Ye Sleepy Souls, Arise*. These two pieces were local carols, and until a few years before, they had sung another local one, the Withy carol. Lastly, the *pièce de résistance* came, *While Shepherds Watched*, to the tune Lyneham. I have never heard carol singing like it; it was so sincere. It could have been the first Christmas.

On New Year's Eve the ringers rang the old year out with a buff or muffled peal, Old Stocky having had to climb among the bells to fix the

The village bellringers

leather mufflers. When the New Year came in, a merry peal was rung and the ringers fired the bells, ringing them all at once like the guns in the 1812 Overture.

Millie Bostock, after carols had been sung at turned midnight, invited the ringers through her house, the darkest, Job Wheatcroft, first, and with wine and mince pies warmed them and wished them a Happy New Year.

11

Looking Back

It has often been said that when we look back over the years the pleasant things are what we remember most. My youth was full of a sense of security. Nothing seemed to change, except the seasons.

Changes were often so gradual that they weren't noticed at the time. The thin end of the wedge describes it. Blenheim, back bent, his cord trousers yorked up, was hoeing sprouts down the Groaten when he remarked to me, 'This parish stinks a sprouts.'

'What's going in that field next year, Blenheim?' I said.

'Oi, sprouts agin like enough. What else can our gaffer plant? It's no good planting wait (wheat). You can buy it at seven bob a hundred at Brown's at Asum. I'll be dalled if we shaunt all look like sprouts.'

'How much wait a thee fayther planted this year, Frederick?' he added. I had to admit only one acre in the Thurness and this was cone wheat, a bearded variety. If we had planted any other sort the sparrows would have eaten the lot. This was in the late twenties and was the only wheat that year in the parish. We grew it for the straw to thatch the hay ricks. Tom Wheatcroft treated the straw like gold and littered the cattle yard in winter with rough hay.

Stocky Hill had to turn from the yearly routine of corn growing to pea hoeing and keeping the pigeons off the sprouts with his twelve-bore gun in winter. Stocky was getting old now but he could still shoot. 'I a just shot a rabbit,' he said. 'Too close. I blowed his yud all of a mommy' (pulp).

This change-over to vegetable growing meant a lot of heavy land was either sown down to grass from arable or, as Tom said, 'fell down', to become turf by grazing and mowing and some basic slag sown by hand broadcast. Slag sowing was a filthy job and the fine particles got on the chest and caused bronchitis. This killed one of the Bradfields. Dr Overthrow said that had he drunk plenty of cider while slag sowing, he would have lived.

The increase in market gardening brought with it a demand for a lighter-legged type of horse. The massive shire horses of the corn farms were too big and too slow for working the horse-hoes up the sprout and pea rows and good half-legged nags were tailored for the job. Handy nags stepped with their smaller hooves in between the plants. They also fitted the bill for horse rakes in the hay fields and taking the milk to the station on dray or float.

Syd Hungerford, who followed Mr Woods whatever at Higford House, brought with him some real shire horses, the last young ones we saw in the village. Tom Wheatcroft told me he could raise a horse up from a screw (a bad doer). I remember one such pony he bought for a fiver in Gloucester market which, by his art and know-how, he made into the finest animal I ever saw go up our village, old Syd sitting in his tub, reins loose, apparently doing nothing. Syd carried certain herbs in his pockets. The smell attracted and he could catch any horse. His son tells me he kept the secret till his death.

But what of our horses (or Walt's)? They seemed like old soldiers; they simply faded away. The day the tractor came, a Fordson with an Oliver plough, there was a quietness among the old men which could almost be felt. Our clay ground had taken four horses on a single-furrow plough; this paraffin job pulled a two-furrow plough.

That autumn Bert Wheatcroft, Tom's son, started ploughing where the peas and beans had been, and even the old shepherd admitted he was doing a fairish job. It was Tom this time who was dubious. The first field was finished and Walt ploughed the headlands with his four remaining horses. Tom said, 'I've sin some of this caper when I was at Higford House. Thee wait till we gets some rain.' Rain came and these being days before hydraulics, the Old Girl, as Bert called his tractor, dug herself in and Walt pulled him out with his 'osses' and the plough was left in the furrow. As the weeks passed and the field was waterlogged the tractor had a melancholy look in the barn. Bert had his leg pulled.

'When bist a gwain to finish ploughing the Thurness?' Walt said,

'Too wet,' said Bert. 'It'll pad the ground.'

Tom came into the barn. 'Oi,' he said. 'I a-knowed the time when I was carter for old Freddy. I was only nineteen year old when we kept guntly (gently) on all the winter at plough, the winter a'mus (almost) half filling the furrows and thy contraption a bin in yer a fortnit tomorrow.' Bert got going again when the weather took up and a good job he did.

Turpin, our foremost horse at plough, was always fond of apples and he went down with the gripes after breaking through into the Tythe Court Orchard and filling himself with Bramley seedlings. I had the unthankful task of walking him up and down the road and not letting him lie down. 'Half a turpentine and half a linsid oil', Tom drenched him with. He got a

A farm labourer from the area

bit better after a few visits from the vet, but his teeth were going and he went, as Walt put it, 'as wake (weak) as a robin'. I shed a tear when the knacker man shot him outside the nag stable and the old shepherd said, 'I s'pose that's another to gu in Spaldings's meat and bone manure.' There is something sad about the end of a faithful horse. It's like the felling of some ancient tree. Turpin was winched up on to the slaughterer's lorry; 'It's no good thee a-snivelling, Fred,' said Walt. 'Sometimes young osses'll die. Old osses be bound to.'

Although Bert did the ploughing with the tractor, Walt still hauled the hay with the horses after Bert had cut the mowing grass, the local blacksmith converting the mowing machine so that the tractor could pull it with Walt on the mowing machine seat. The horses went as Turpin went, most of them completing their allotted span of about twenty-five to thirty years. I liked to go in Boss Close on a summer Sunday afternoon and watch the horses, rolling on the grass, sometimes lying stretched out in the sun. Bonnie lived to thirty-two, outliving Turpin, her eldest son.

And then the men, the corner-stones of my childhood, suddenly seemed old and frail and mortal. Joe Baker just slipped away, aged nearly ninety, while I was on holiday one summer. Tom Wheatcroft, who in his younger days could carry a two-and-a-quarter-hundredweight sack of wheat up anywhere, told me he had got so that he could just about carry the empty sack. 'I was born too soon. That's my trouble,' he said.

Changes came too with the Depression, but in 1930, when the poor and unemployed suffered extreme hardship in the towns and cities, the countryside under Bredon was relatively better off. Here the employers were strict in an almost Victorian way, but they kept their men. There was almost full employment. Smallholders led a precarious life, dependent on wind and weather, drought and flood, to make a return on their crops, to give a little margin over expenses. Farmers took to market gardening or turned to stock raising. The farmworker after paying his rent had little left to buy the sevenpence-an-ounce Red Bell tobacco, but grew potatoes on field headlands, scrogged the apple orchards after the pickers had finished and stored enough for winter dumplings. When a man is on the breadline he improvises. The first few motor cars of the immigrant insurance men, dentists and retired Army officers, often gave a lift to the Saturday shopper who could ill afford Mr Anderson's bus or the train to Evesham. The men bought meat from the Argentine at a little shop up Port Street, Evesham, beef at fourpence a pound if they waited late on a Saturday night, and they walked home with a full frail. Fresh vegetables were always available as the sprout fields spread from the Vale of Evesham to Bredon Hill and beyond.

173

By working hard Jimmy Blizzard's sons could earn ten shillings a day picking for market. It is not true to say that the years of the Depression were not felt in our village because for a honeymoon period after the First War, wages and conditions had been reasonable. The Midnight Milkman made his two rounds a day with his milk but now some folk turned to buying skimmed milk from Kate Dunn who made butter for market, some bought cheap condensed milk. Every week in the season of colder weather when the rabbits squatted on their grassy forms on Bredon Hill, men carried stones or a hammer in their grey fustian working coat to throw at the rabbits on their way to and from work. Most cottagers had a stew jar on the hob or in the oven with a turnip from the sheepfold, a few carrots and onions which made a mid-week meal for the family.

A farmer, some years retired, did a bit of fruit picking to earn his rates as his shares went down.

But as Stodge chewed his twist then dried it in his tobacco tin to smoke later and men robbed partridges' nests for eggs, shot wood pigeons for meat, there was a satisfaction. I am sure that the village folk were reasonably content. There was little money for clothes but to see Jimmy Blizzard on a Sunday in Tiddley Stidiford the artist's cast-off suit was a sight to remember. Tiddley was a tall man with a long body, Jimmy was short and square. The trousers reached almost to his armpits and his braces held them there. Even then the turnups of the Haris tweed were well down on his boots. The women fitted themselves up at rummage sales but the children often had their clothes handed down in the family, and to see a well-dressed child in 1930 was a rarity. Boys of fourteen left school for the plough driving, but the ones that got away went by cycle to Evesham as apprentice hairdressers or lather boys.

It was fortunate that there was full employment on the land, for the agricultural labourer could draw no dole, only sickness benefit.

The people I knew 'made a good staddle to build on', as Tom Wheatcroft would have put it. They knew their Ayshon (Ashton). They loved it. They studied it. If you asked them the way to Campden, they possibly could not have told you. But they knew the Rabbit Lane at Beckford where Spring-Heeled Jack was supposed to meet the White Lady on moonlight nights. They talked of Bobbity Lantern's 'Will o' the Wisps' in the Dewrest by Carrants Brook. Or the Cuckoo Pen on Little Hill. This group of beech trees still stands. I wonder whether Squire Bostock had anything to do with this? You see, the old idea of penning the cuckoo was that by keeping him enclosed all winter and not letting him return to southern lands, they could keep with him a state of perpetual spring and summer.